STYLE MANUAL

FOR

ESSAYS AND THESES

PAUL HAFFNER

GRACEWING

First published as
A Methodology for Term papers and Theses in 1996 by
Gracewing
2, Southern Avenue
Leominster
HerefordshireHR6 0QF
www.gracewing.co.uk

New edition 2010, revised, updated, enlarged and reset.

ISBN 978 085244 743 7

Cover: Strahov Monastery Library, Prague

TABLE OF CONTENTS

INTRODUCTION

This little book is a short guide to essential style and method for writing papers and theses in the Roman ecclesiastical faculties and universities. It is not exhaustive, but simply furnishes the main elements of a method which should help the student to make a consistent series of references and a coherent bibliography as well as producing a scientifically respectable text. It could also prove useful to authors of academic books.

My manual is based on my own experience in writing a doctoral dissertation as well as other books and papers. It takes into account my experience in marking various pieces of written work, where I have been able to see the main pitfalls and problems which the student encounters. The method provided here is congruent with that used in documents of the Pope and the Congregations of the Roman Curia, as well as with those approaches employed in various pontifical universities. It should also be useful elsewhere *mutatis mutandis,* and in subjects other than philosophy and theology. This work regards method as a means rather than as an end and so the student should be able to see the wood for the trees. It does not 'legislate' on details of typography or page layout, since more and more students are using computers, in which a word-processing package arranges automatically what previously had to be thought out with a typewriter. It is my hope that the student would be able to adapt it where necessary to his or her particular needs. The choice of a methodology allows freedom, for any consistent method is acceptable. However, this choice is not arbitrary, since some forms of methodology lend themselves more easily to a logical application. It is to be hoped that the present volume contains a straightforward and logical approach. This book owes much to Tom Longford and Jo Ratcliffe whose generous help brought it to birth.

Rome, 1 May 1996
Feast of St. Joseph the Worker

PREFACE TO NEW EDITION

After nearly fifteen years, I have decided to publish a considerably extended version of my text dealing with the mechanics of writing essays, term papers and academic theses. My reasons for a new edition are manifold. First, over the past twenty years computer science and information technology have made great strides forward. These advances have been a double-edged sword for the academic world, presenting both opportunities and dangers. Opportunities, because the computer has become an important tool in the storage and elaboration of research data. Dangers, because the mass of information available on the Internet is, to say the least, of variable quality. In any case, it is necessary to take these changes into account, both regarding the technicalities of storing research data, and the methods of citing these data in a scholarly way.

Next, while the earlier version of this manual dealt with academic papers and theses in philosophical and theological disciplines, the current version embraces the humanities and liberal arts, and also albeit briefly, takes account of the natural sciences. I have taken into consideration the approaches of the Chicago style manual, of the Modern Humanities Research Association, of the American Psychological Association, of the *MLA Handbook for Writers of Research Papers*, and of the Institute of Electrical and Electronics Engineers, as well as of several others. In the final analysis, while there are elements common to all style methods, my own differs from that of the others to make it unique, but it is sufficiently related to the other approaches not to be regarded as eccentric. Of course it deals only with a method specific to writing in the English language.

Finally, while not wishing to inflate the text so that it overawes the student, I felt it was also appropriate to adds some material on stylistic and grammatical issues. I hope that this renewed text will continue to be of service to the many students who are trying to make headway in their research and writing as well as to writers who need to adopt a consistent method in preparing their books.

Rome, 1 July 2010
Feast of the Precious Blood

1 STUDY SKILLS

These studies are an impetus to youth, and a delight to age; they are an adornment to good fortune, refuge and relief in trouble; they enrich private life and do not hamper public life; they are with us by night, they are with us on long journeys, they are with us in the depths of the country.

Cicero, *Pro Archia*, VII, 16

Mysterious machines are the exclusive products of science-fiction writers.

Stanley Jaki, *Brain, Mind and Computers*

1.1 Sources

Writing papers, articles, theses or books involves the technique of consulting various types of sources. These sources form the raw material from which the final product is shaped, so great care should be exercised in excavating the various mines of information. Collecting and collating material forms the important basis of the first stage of any research activity.

1.1.1 Libraries

Normally the required books, periodicals, video, audio, microfiche, rare titles and even archive material will be found in university libraries, but sometimes it may be necessary to approach a more specialized collection. Many libraries have 'special collections' departments which hold materials which are, for example, rare, valuable or fragile. These departments often operate in a similar manner to archives. If you wish to consult this type of material it is necessary to contact the library concerned in advance to check the access policy for these collections. It is unlikely that any one library will be able to provide you with all the resources you require. You may need to access a variety of repositories, ranging from other academic libraries to archives, museums or government libraries. Your research may even take you abroad. The conditions on which libraries will allow access to readers can vary enormously. Readers can save themselves time by learning the system which is used to catalogue the books and periodicals. The older method was a system of index cards arranged according to the author or the title of a given book or periodical. Each book or periodical is numbered, and the library is organized according to these numbers. Now most library cataloguing systems have been updated on computers. In the event of any particular difficulty, a librarian should be approached.

1.1.2 Archives

Here an archivist will find the required material, so he or she should be furnished with a clear idea of the date and content of what is being sought after. Archives are often organized according to the position number, which relates to the topic of the material, and the protocol number which determines the particular document you are dealing with. The protocol number usually consists of a figure and a date. For example 3626/84 is the three thousand and twenty-sixth document classified in the year 1984. Elsewhere, the serial number of the manuscript (MS 40) and the folio number (f.26) are used. These are not the only methods for arranging archives, so the researcher should try and understand a little of the system of any collection consulted. The relevant parameters should be taken down, as they will be required for citation in the references. Also, it may be necessary to consult the material another time, something is missed on the first attempt. It will greatly help the archivist if the researcher can quote the parameters of the required document. Permission should be sought from the archivist in order that the material consulted may be quoted in a text, especially if this is to be published, since archive material may be confidential or classified.

1.1.3 Interviews

Interviews and questionnaires should not be employed unless absolutely necessary, for academic written work is different from journalism. Conducting a survey and analysing the results constitutes an advanced series of scientific skills which may well prove very time-consuming. In a piece of philosophical or theological written work, the primary sources would rarely be the results of a survey. It may be better to consult the results of a survey which has already been processed and analysed. However if this type of source is employed, the purpose of the interview should be made clear to the interviewee and his or her written permission should be obtained to quote the results in the write-up. The interviewee should be carefully recorded on a suitable audio system. It would also be correct, once the first draft of the work has been written, to ask the interviewee to see if they are satisfied with the way they have been quoted and to verify that their thought has not been distorted. This verification process may be difficult or even impossible if there are a very large number of people interviewed. It will be necessary to state in the written work the nature of the medium on which the material gathered during interviews was recorded, or whether it was simply written down. This material should be kept, as it may be needed later to defend what has been written.

1.1.4 The Internet

Clearly, more and more students are turning to the Internet when doing research for their assignments, and more and more teachers are permitting or encouraging this research when setting topics. Apart from the problem of plagiarism, research on the Net is very different from traditional library research, and these differences can cause problems. The Net can be a useful resource, but it must be used carefully and critically. First, one should distinguish between a printed resource which has been scanned onto a webpage, but not cross-checked to avoid typographical mistakes, and a resource which is reliable because it has been photographed into file form.

The printed resources you find in a library have almost always been thoroughly evaluated by experts before they are published. This process of 'peer review' is the difference between an article in a news magazine and one in a learned journal such as *Gregorianum* or *Nature*.[1] Furthermore, when books and other materials come into a university library system, they are painstakingly and systematically catalogued and cross-referenced using procedures followed by research libraries the world over. This process is the basis for the way materials are

1. Scholarly *peer review* is the process of subjecting an author's scholarly work, research, or ideas to the scrutiny of others who are experts in the same field. Peer review requires a community of experts in a given field, who are qualified and able to perform impartial review. Impartial review, especially of work in less narrowly defined or inter-disciplinary fields, may be difficult to accomplish; and the significance of an idea may never be widely appreciated among its contemporaries. Peer review can render the ability to publish susceptible to control by elites and to personal jealousy. The peer review process may also suppress dissent against so-called 'mainstream' theories. Reviewers tend to be especially critical of conclusions that contradict their own views, and lenient towards those that accord with them.

organized in the library, and it makes possible the various search functions of the electronic catalogue.

On the Internet, on the other hand, almost anything goes. Anyone can put anything they want on a Web site, there is no review or screening process, and there are no universally agreed standard ways of identifying subjects and creating cross-references. This is both the glory and the weakness of the Net—it's either freedom or chaos, depending on your point of view, and this means that you have to pay close attention when doing research online. There are a great many solid academic resources available on the Net, including hundreds of on-line journals and sites set up by universities and scholarly or scientific organizations. Using material from those sources is no problem; it's just like going to the library, only on-line. It's all the other material on the Net that you have to be cautious about.

A few basic guidelines should be borne in mind. First, you should not rely exclusively on Net resources. Sometimes your assignment will be to do research only in the library, but often your instructors will expect you to make use of both Internet and library resources. Cross-checking information from the Net against information from the library is a good way to make sure that the Net material is reliable and authoritative.

You need to narrow your research topic before logging on. The Internet allows access to so much information that you can easily be overwhelmed. Before you start your search, think about what you're looking for, and, if possible, formulate some very specific questions to direct and limit your search.

It is crucial to know your subject directories and search engines. There are several high quality peer-reviewed subject directories containing links selected by subject experts. These are suitable places to start your academic research on the Internet. Other search engines differ considerably in how they work, how much of the Net they search, and the kind of results you can expect to obtain from them. Spending some time learning what each search engine will do and how best to use it can help you avoid a lot of frustration and wasted time later. Because each one will find different things for you, it's a good idea to use always more than one search engine.

Keep a detailed record of sites you visit and the sites you use. Doing research on the Net inevitably means visiting some sites that are useful and many that are not. Keeping track is necessary so that you can revisit the useful ones later, and also put the required references in your paper. Don't just rely on your browser's history function, because it retains the Web addresses or URLs of all the sites you visit: if you're using a public or shared computer, the memory in the history file will be erased at the end of your session.[2] It's better to write down or bookmark the sites you've found useful, so that you'll have a permanent record.

Double-check all URLs that you put in your written work. It's easy to make mistakes with complicated Internet addresses, and errors will make your references useless. To be safe, type them into the location box of your browser and check that they take you to the correct site. The following points are guidelines for evaluating specific resources you find on the Net. If you use this checklist when looking at a website, you can avoid many errors and problems.

2. In computing, a *Uniform Resource Locator* (URL) is a *Uniform Resource Identifier* (URI) that specifies where an identified resource is available and the mechanism for retrieving it. The best-known example of a URL is the 'address' of a webpage on the World Wide Web, for example http://www.gracewing.co.uk.

Authority

You need to evaluate the authority of a given website. First you need to see who the author is, if his name is given. You need to check his qualifications, and see whether he is an authority in the area under consideration. You need to verify if the author has been cited elsewhere (in class, or in your course text or in library material). You need to ascertain if the author has written elsewhere on this topic.

Affiliation

The next step is to determine the affiliation of the website. It is important to find out who is the sponsor of the website, and to check whether the author is affiliated with a reputable institution or organization. Moreover, you need to ask whether the information reflects the views of the organization, or only of the author. If the sponsoring institution or organization is not clearly identified on the site, check the URL. It may contain the name of a university or the extension '.edu', which is used by many educational institutions. Government sites are identified by the extension '.gov'. URLs containing '.org' are trickier, and require research: these are sites sponsored by non-profit organizations, some of which are reliable sources and some of which are very biased. Sites with the '.com' extension should also be used with caution, because they have commercial or corporate sponsors who probably want to sell you something. Then there are personal webpages with no institutional backing; use such sites only if you have checked on the author's credibility in print sources.

Audience level

Next you should consider at which audience level the website is pitched. You require information at the university or research level. Don't use sites intended for elementary students or else sites that are too advanced or too technical for your needs.

Up to date?

You need to determine whether the website is current or else out of date. You can verify this by looking at the date of the most recent update, if it is given. Generally speaking, Internet resources should be up-to-date; after all, getting the most current information is the main reason for doing Net research in the first place. You need to check if all the links are up-to-date and working. Broken links may mean the site is out-of-date; they're certainly a sign that it's not well-maintained.

Reliability and accuracy

You need to ascertain whether the material on the website is reliable and accurate, whether it is factual, and not purely opinion. You need to see whether you can verify the information in print sources. The source of the information should be clearly stated, whether it be original research material or secondary material obtained from elsewhere. With the help of your teacher, you should check the validity of the research at its source, and whether the material, as presented, has substance and depth. You should analyse the arguments presented, to see if they are based on strong evidence and good logic, and whether the author's point of view is impartial and objective. A telling sign of the professional touch is when the site is free of errors in spelling or grammar and other evidence of carelessness in its presentation of the material. A further positive sign is furnished by additional electronic and print sources provided to complement or support the material on the website.

If you can answer most of these questions positively when looking at a particular site, then you can be pretty sure it's a good one; if it doesn't measure up one way or another, it's probably a site to avoid. The key to the whole process is to think critically about what you find on the Net; if you want to use it, you are responsible for determining whether it is reliable and accurate.

1.2 The use of computers

1.2.1 Basic rules

It is wise never to spend too long at one session working with a computer as this can tire the eyes. The correct bodily posture should also be maintained when working at a video-terminal.

Work carried out on a computer should always be saved regularly, so that if there is a power cut, and there is no protective device on the system, a large quantity of material will not be lost. Most programs automatically make a back-up copy of each document; this setting is always preferable, so that if the computer should close down unexpectedly (even because of a virus), one can recuperate as much data as possible.

A backup disk should be kept of all the work carried out, and this must be continually updated by saving to disk the new work completed by the end of a morning or afternoon of writing. In this way, if material on the hard disk becomes corrupted, the risk of losing precious hours of work will be avoided. It is also wise to keep a printout (hard copy) of the work as it proceeds.

If the work is written with a word-processing package on a computer, much of what used to be done on a typewriter is automatically carried out by the program itself. Within a chosen standard paper size (such as A4) the computer program has customizable left and right margins, top and bottom margins, and line-spacing yielding a set page length (often around 25 lines per double-spaced A4 page). The program also arranges where the page numbers are placed and performs more complex functions such as the organization of footnotes and end notes. It is important to make the most of the program to obtain from it the final page layout that is desired. In general, it is better to utilize a simple software package which is suitable for the particular needs which the researcher encounters in the job at hand, rather than a system which is highly sophisticated, but which will be more trouble than it is worth.

Hardware and software should be matched. In other words the word-processing package should be matched with the particular printer that is connected to the computer. Otherwise various characters may come out in a strange way, or else the page length may not be correct. Particular issues can arise with biblical languages like Greek and Hebrew. Also, it is sometimes necessary to experiment with page length and margins so that the page is printed as it appears on the screen or at least as desired. Matching is also necessary to obtain the kind of print or typeface that is required. Most word-processing packages come supplied with several print fonts.

The keyboard and mouse of the computer should cleaned occasionally, so that any build up of dust or foreign matter is avoided. Only cleaning products especially sold for computers should be adopted. An anti-virus system and a firewall should be employed to check that no unwanted guests are present in the system! Movable data storage devices such as USB flash drives and other external drives should never be accepted from unknown sources.[3]

---

3. A USB flash drive consists of a flash memory data storage device integrated with a USB (Universal Serial Bus) 1.1 or 2.0 interface. USB flash drives are typically removable and rewritable, and physically much smaller than a floppy disk.

1.2.2 Practical points

Widows and orphans should be avoided as far as possible. An *orphan* occurs when the first line of a paragraph appears alone at the bottom of a page. It also happens when a title or subtitle within a text is placed right at the bottom of a page and then the text to which it refers is on the next page. In other words, the title is orphaned from its text. The title should be moved onto the next page to accompany its text. A *widow* occurs when the last few words of a paragraph lie alone at the top of a page, so that these words are widowed from their sentence. These few words should be put on the previous page, or else, if this is not possible, the whole sentence should be placed on the next page.

A check should be made to ensure that the computer program makes correctly hyphenated line-breaks for the language employed in the piece of written work. A problem can arise in this respect if an Italian or Spanish word-processing package is being used, but the written work is in English.

Care should be taken that the right margin of the page is 'justified' for papers and theses. A justified text has all lines the same length so that its right edge, as well as its left edge, is straight. A 'ragged' right edge may be acceptable for a letter, but not in academic written work.[4] Similarly it should be ensured that a line doesn't

---

Most weigh less than 30 g with storage capacities (as of 2010) as large as 256 GB.

4. In American usage, a ragged right edge (or a left-aligned margin) is most often acceptable for a term paper, and it is considered more informal, friendlier than justified text. It may, however, require extra attention to hyphenation to keep right margin from being too ragged. Generally, though, setting margins left-aligned is easier to work with, requiring less time, attention, and adjustment from the student to make it look good.

begin with punctuation, which should have appeared at the end of the previous line. This happens when a space has been left between the last letter of a sentence and the punctuation mark; in this case, the justification mechanism of the computer program can throw the punctuation mark down to the next line.

It may seem elementary, but care should be taken to see that the pages of any piece of written work are numbered. Many word-processing programs are set with a default for omitting page numbering. So it is worthwhile to check that page numbers and all other necessary elements are present in the written work by having a look at the page preview system which allows the writer to view the pages as they will actually appear when they are printed.

1.2.3 Research tools

It is wise to keep up-to-date on information technology as far as finances permit. With the electronic transmission of data and scanning techniques, it is possible to import written passages from the sources into the written work, saving the need for keying-in large blocks of text. This can be a great time saver. There are also several programs which assist the researcher in making notes and bibliography. Remember, though, that no electronic aid can replace the 3 'I's' of research, namely, inspiration, intuition and imagination.

Scholar's Aid

Scholar's Aid (found at www.scholarsaid.com) was first created in 1996 by a seminarian who wanted to organize his bibliography and found that existing bibliographical software was expensive and did not meet his needs. He was a computer programmer with twenty years experience, and he therefore decided to develop superior (and cheaper) software to meet both his own needs and the needs of the hundreds of thousands of other students and scholars who had similar needs. Scholar's Aid keeps bibliographical data and notes together, for the very good reason that scholars always need to keep their notes linked to the sources from which those notes were made. Indeed, in academic writing, scholars constantly support their argument by reference to the sources on which they have worked. Thus, in directly quoting from one of these sources, or in making reference to another's ideas, rigorous academic scholarship demands accurate and detailed citation of those original sources. Scholar's Aid automates this process in a manner that is entirely without precedent. Provided the original notes were written in the Notes module of Scholar's Aid, by selecting text and clicking one of the transfer buttons, the program transfers the selected text into the word-processed document and, at exactly the same time, inserts an appropriate citation into the document in a form (footnote, short footnote, endnote, short endnote and parenthetical reference) determined by the user. The program even includes the correct page number in the citation that it creates within the word-processed document.

The WebNote feature of Scholar's Aid allows you to store the contents of web pages in your notes. You can store whole pages including sounds and pictures, just as you would if you saved a web page in your web browser. Using WebNote you can make a link to the source in the Library module. WebNote will store the original Internet URL so it can be easily updated or refreshed as required.

The Library module of Scholar's Aid is used to store and organize bibliographical data drawn from a wide range of sources (books, articles, Internet websites, and the like). This information is linked to the notes in the Notes module and then you can generate the most common forms of references (full and short footnotes, full and short parenthetical references, bibliographical entries and reference list items). These references can then be transferred automatically to documents loaded in a word-processor by issuing a simple menu command or by clicking a button. The format of the resulting reference can conform to one of the standard styles supplied with the package (Chicago and APA), or to a style designed by users to meet their own specific requirements.

Users can import external references because Scholar's Aid 4AE is compliant with the Z39.50 protocol.[5] Users can use any of the more than 100 server definitions that are provided with the program or add extras. Also, users can import data from an Endnote® exported text file as well as accessing data like styles, libraries, and records in any other application. The User Manager feature of Scholar's Aid 4AE allows users to have independent user interface settings. A user's data can be stored in different folders.

Bibus

Bibus (found at bibus-biblio.sourceforge.net) is a free bibliographic and reference management software. As with other similar tools, Bibus allows one to search, edit, and sort bibliographic records. In addition, Bibus contains features that makes it unique among open source and even commercial bibliographic databases. The main interface of Bibus should be intuitive for anybody used to a email reader. On the left there is a tree with keys.

5. Z39.50 is a client–server protocol for searching and retrieving information from remote computer databases. The standard's maintenance agency is the US Library of Congress. Z39.50 is widely used in library environments and is often incorporated into integrated library systems and personal bibliographic reference software. Interlibrary catalogue searches for interlibrary loan are often implemented with Z39.50 queries.

Each key is associated with a list of references. When the key is selected, the references associated with this key are listed in the list view located on the top panel of the right side of the window. When a reference is selected in this list, this reference is shown at the bottom right of the window. It allows hierarchical organization of the references with user-defined keys, and is designed for multiuser environments, whereby one can share the database between an 'unlimited' number of users. Each user will have its own classification. Live queries are possible, namely searches that update as the database changes. Bibus enables the insertion of references and formatting of bibliographies into two widely used word-processors, namely OpenOffice.org and Microsoft Word. A number of specific styles are available, as well as the possibility of creating further custom styles.

Mendeley

Mendeley (found at www.mendeley.com) is an example of a web-based research tool. There are two components to the Mendeley system. The software on your local computer, Mendeley Desktop, and the storage on the Internet, Mendeley Web. You can use Mendeley Desktop independently of the Mendeley Web component, but a free account obtains 500MB of online storage for your documents for remote access, synchronizing across computers, and with document backup. *Mendeley Desktop* organizes your research paper collection and citations. It automatically extracts references from documents, generates bibliographies, and is freely available on Windows, Mac OS X and Linux. *Mendeley Web* lets you access your research paper library from anywhere, share documents in closed groups, and collaborate on research projects online. It connects you to like-minded academics and puts the latest research trend statistics at your fingertips.

Mendeley Desktop lets the researcher set up his personal research paper database from multiple sources. Mendeley Desktop automatically extracts bibliographic data, keywords, and cited references from PDFs (Portable Document Format files) and turns them into a searchable full-text database. Just drag and drop PDFs into Mendeley Desktop to start the automatic extraction of bibliographic metadata (authors, year, journal, volume, issue, and so forth). Mendeley's algorithms scan the PDF full-text, as well as using XMP metadata where available, turning a collection of research papers into a structured, sortable database.[6] Mendeley detects subject keywords within your PDFs, indexes the full-text for quick searching across all documents, and even extracts each research papers' cited references. There is one-click citation import from Google Scholar and PubMed: thus one can add documents and references from more than 50 academic databases with a single click. Mendeley cross-checks your research paper collection against external databases like CrossRef, PubMed, arXiv, or Google Scholar, using DOIs (Digital Object Identifier Systems) and other unique identifiers. When additional information, such as abstracts and keywords, are available, they are automatically added to your research paper library.

It is possible to import from and synchronize with other reference managers. If you desire to use various bibliography and citation tools, Mendeley imports and exports the most important bibliography data formats

6. The Adobe *Extensible Metadata Platform* (XMP) is a standard, created by Adobe Systems, for processing and storing standardized and proprietary information relating to the contents of a file. XMP standardizes the definition, creation, and processing of extensible metadata. Embedding metadata avoids many problems that occur when metadata is stored separately. XMP is used in PDF, photography and photo editing applications.

and synchronizes with several browser-based citation-capturing tools, so you can keep your existing work flow and benefit from each tool's strengths. Mendeley imports your existing BibTex, RIS, and EndNote™ XML libraries. These bibliography file formats are supported by EndNote, Reference Manager™, RefWorks™, and other traditional reference management tools. Mendeley Desktop can continuously sync with your existing CiteULike and Zotero libraries. Whenever you add a citation there, it appears in your Mendeley library seconds later—so you can manage and backup everything in one place.

One can generate bibliographies in more than 1,000 different citation styles, including Association for Computing Machinery (ACM), American Chemical Society (ACS), American Medical Association (AMA), American Psychological Association (APA), Chicago Manual of Style, Elsevier, Harvard Reference Format, IEEE, Modern Language Association (MLA), National Library of Medicine, Nature, Public Library of Science (PLoS), or Science.

Mendeley generates reference lists for you, in over 1,000 different citation styles. Mendeley comes with citation generator plugins for Microsoft Word and OpenOffice. The researcher can thus insert citations from the research paper library. If one is using LaTeX to write papers, Mendeley can automatically generate an always-up-to-date collection of BibTex entries that is synchronized to the relevant PDF research paper collection.[7] The student can insert formatted citation lists

7. LaTeX is a document markup language and document preparation system for the TeX typesetting program. The term LaTeX refers only to the language in which documents are written, not to the editor used to write those documents. In order to create a document in LaTeX, a .tex file must be created using some form of text editor. While most text editors can be used to create a LaTeX document, a number of edi-

into any text editor, including Google Docs, blogs, or e-mails, simply by dragging and dropping a reference from Mendeley to the text editor.

Mendeley is a convenient way to set up a shared library for your team and for specific research projects —your documents, tags, and annotations stay synchronized. You can also set up public research paper collections and subscribe to updates. Moreover, Mendeley lets you build your academic profile for others to discover your areas of expertise, and you can create your personal network of research contacts for current and future research collaboration. The system enables you to discover the most important papers, authors and topics in your discipline—right now and in real-time. Mendeley is fast becoming one of the biggest research databases in the world—and the only one with a layer of social information about the readership demographics and user-generated tags for each research paper. Mendeley gives you powerful real-time insight into trends in research.

---

tors have been created specifically for working with LaTeX. LaTeX is most widely used by mathematicians, scientists, engineers, philosophers, linguists, economists and other scholars in academia. As a primary or intermediate format, like translating DocBook and other XML-based formats to PDF, LaTeX is used because of the high quality of typesetting achievable by TeX. The typesetting system offers programmable desktop publishing features and extensive facilities for automating most aspects of typesetting and desktop publishing, including numbering and cross-referencing, tables and figures, page layout and bibliographies.

1.3 Scientific Research

1.3.1 Reading

Creative and successful writing depends on reading with critical understanding. Most of the papers you write will involve reflection on written texts, constituting the thinking and research that has already been done on your subject. In order to write your own analysis of this subject, you will need to do careful critical reading of sources and to employ them critically to form your own argument. The judgments and interpretations you make of the texts you read are the first steps towards formulating your own approach.

To read in an intelligent manner is to make judgements about how a text is argued. This is a highly reflective skill requiring you to 'stand back' and gain some distance from the text you are reading. You might have to read a text through once to get a basic grasp of content before you launch into an intensive critical reading. In other words, one is not reading solely to collect information, but also to develop ways of thinking about the subject matter. When you are reading, highlighting, or taking notes, avoid extracting and compiling lists of evidence, lists of facts and examples. Avoid approaching a text by asking only 'What information can I get out of it?' Rather ask 'How does this text work? How is it argued? How is the evidence (the facts, examples, and so forth) used and interpreted? How does the text reach its conclusions?'

The first step is to determine the central claims or purpose of the text, or its main thesis. A critical reading attempts to assess how these central claims are developed or argued. Next one needs to make some judgements about context, in order to determine the audience for whom the text was written, and the other scholars or authors (maybe with differing viewpoints) with whom the text is in dialogue. The historical context has to be examined in order to contribute to your assessment of what is going on in a text.

Then you need to distinguish the kinds of reasoning the text employs. Here you need to examine the concepts which are defined and used, to see if the text appeals to a given theory or school of thought. If there is an appeal to a particular concept, theory, or method, you need to see how that concept, theory, or method is then used to organize and interpret the data. You should determine the author's specific methodology, and also examine how the text is organized: in other words you see how the author has analysed and synthesised the material. Be aware that different disciplines (like theology, history, sociology, philosophy, biology) will have different ways of arguing.

The next step is to examine the evidence (the supporting facts, examples, and so forth) which the text employs. Supporting evidence is indispensable to an argument. Your evaluation of what counts as evidence in this argument is necessary to classify the evidence according to whether it is theological, legal, statistical, literary, historical, or scientific. Then organize the sources from which the evidence is taken, and determine whether these sources are primary or secondary.

Critical reading involves evaluation. Your reading of a text is already critical if it accounts for and makes a series of judgments about how a text is argued. However, some essays may also require you to assess the strengths and weaknesses of an argument. If the argument is strong, you should be able to detail why it is strong, and ask whether it could be better or differently supported. You need to be able to identify gaps, leaps, or inconsistencies in the argument. It is necessary to examine the underlying assumptions and method of analysis, to see if they are problematic. You should ask whether the evidence could be interpreted differently, and thus whether the conclusions are warranted by the evidence presented.

Some Practical Tips

1. Critical reading occurs after some preliminary processes of reading. Begin by skimming research materials, especially introductions and conclusions, in order to choose strategically where to focus your critical efforts.
2. When highlighting a text or taking notes from it, teach yourself to highlight arguments: those places in a text where an author explains his analytical moves, the concepts he uses, how he uses them, how he arrives at conclusions. Don't let yourself only highlight facts and examples, no matter how interesting they may be. First, look for the large patterns that give purpose, order, and meaning to those examples. The opening sentences of paragraphs can be important to this task.
3. When you begin to think about how you might use a portion of a text in the argument you are forging in your own paper, try to remain aware of how this portion fits into the whole argument from which it is taken. Paying attention to context is a fundamental critical move.
4. When you quote directly from a source, use the quotation critically. This means that you should not substitute the quotation for your own articulation of a point. Rather, introduce the quotation by laying out the judgments you are making about it, and the reasons why you are using it. Often a quotation is followed by some further analysis.
5. Critical reading skills are also critical listening skills. In your lectures, listen not only for information but

also for ways of thinking. Your instructor will often describe and model ways of thinking appropriate to a discipline.

1.3.2 Primary and secondary sources

Not all sources are equally valid, nor will you necessarily want to use every source available. Read and evaluate your sources to determine which will provide the strongest and most reliable support for your thesis. There is no need to read every source cover to cover; study the table of contents and the index to see if there is anything helpful for your work.

Consider the reliability of your sources and try to determine if the writer has a particular bias. Note how recent the information is. You would not want to write an essay on heart disease by citing a fourteenth-century medical treatise, although such a source would be pertinent to a discussion of the medieval world view. Try to determine how respected and well-received the source is, although you need not necessarily reject sources which challenge established views.

Finally, consider your own reactions to your sources and add these to your notes. Of course, evaluating resources does not mean rejecting anything that contradicts your thesis. A strong paper will acknowledge and account for contradictory evidence.

Evidence consists of specific examples or opinions of others which support and illustrate your essay or thesis. It is advisable to give several examples rather than just one. The writer should make sure that there is sufficient evidence to make a strong point; the evidence must also be relevant, reliable, and representative. Evidence comes from either primary or secondary sources. The primary source is the text on which you are commenting, or documents that deal directly with your topic. Secondary sources are opinions or interpretation of others on the topic; your essay or thesis itself becomes a secondary source, should anyone wish to quote it.

Not every assignment will require you to consult secondary sources. In some courses, professors prefer not to assign research essays involving secondary sources because they want the student to come to his own conclusions about the text. In this kind of essay, a careful rereading of the work or works you are discussing will allow you to develop your ideas more fully, in the way that formal research does for a research essay. If you do consult secondary sources, be sure not to rely too heavily on them. Sometimes these sources will support your topic, other times you will need to adapt your view to suit your sources; avoid the trap of the cut and paste essay that simply collects opinions of others and rearranges them.

Consider the following as traps to avoid when citing secondary sources:

1. Appealing to an authority outside of your field (do not, for example, quote a literary critic on the effectiveness of vitamin C).
2. Misrepresenting the opinions of the authority.
3. Assuming that one quotation in a source is typical of the whole.
4. Citing an authority which has lost authority—check the validity of your authority and make sure the information is up to date (do not quote Ptolemy in a paper on astronomy).

The type of secondary sources you seek out will depend on the assignment. Secondary sources can include biographical material, factual material, definitions, studies, commentaries, criticism , virtually anything you consult outside the original material itself.

One problem writers come up against when completing research assignments is how to use secondary sources and still write something new or relatively 'original'. You might try judging or challenging old ideas, or concentrating on a controversy between sources. Use secondary sources to show that you know what has been said and give your opinion about it. Research is not a substitute for your own careful thought and analysis.

1.3.3 Intellectual honesty

By intellectual honesty, is meant that in any written text, ideas found elsewhere are always acknowledged, stating their precise source. It would be seriously wrong to present as one's own idea what belongs in the work of some other author. Research aims to seek 'the truth, the whole truth and nothing but the truth' and so all the dimensions of truth must be scrupulously respected.

Clearly, scientists and scholars build on the ideas and research of others. Bernard of Chartres used to say that we are like dwarfs on the shoulders of giants, so that we can see more than they, and things at a greater distance, not by virtue of any sharpness of sight on our part, or any physical distinction, but because we are carried high and raised up by their giant size.[8]

Nevertheless, originality is also important in science, as reflected in the harsh academic code of *publish or perish*. Thus scientists and academics of all stripes are punctilious about drawing a clear line between what is original in one's work, and what is not. Since academics are the watchdogs and graders of student writing, it is critically important for students to learn what plagiarism is and what dangers it presents.

---

8. See John of Salisbury, *Metalogicon*, III: 'Dicebat Bernardus Carnotensis nos esse quasi nanos, gigantium humeris insidentes, ut possimus plura eis et remotiora videre, non utique proprii visus acumine, aut eminentia corporis, sed quia in altum subvenimur et extollimur magnitudine gigantea.'

The Random House dictionary defines plagiarism as 'the unauthorized use or close imitation of the language and thoughts of another author and the representation of them as one's own original work'. Imitation or borrowing by themselves are not plagiarism. Drawing on other people's ideas is perfectly reasonable and in fact unavoidable when you write academic essays—but you must acknowledge the borrowing.

You are obliged, as an ethical duty to other writers and as a defence for yourself, to acknowledge all material you take from other sources, even if you do not copy the exact words used in the original—even if you never actually quote the original. Plagiarism includes the following elements:

1. Quoting material without attribution. This is most obvious kind of plagiarism.
2. Passing off another writer's idea as your own, even if it's been reworded. Changing the phrasing of an original does not avoid plagiarism. The underlying idea of plagiarism is unacknowledged borrowing of ideas, not specific words.
3. Imitating the structure or argument of a passage without attribution. Suppose a source presents an assertion and three supporting points. If you adopt that particular structure, including the particular examples or supporting points, you need to provide a citation to the original. This holds even if you substantially revise the wording.
4. Concealing the extent to which you have borrowed from a text or other source. Citing a specific passage in a work doesn't give you license to draw on the rest of the work without citation. This is the craftiest kind of plagiarism.

Questions about ownership of ideas are not always so simple, and this leads to some basic issues. First one cannot avoid problems just by listing every source in the bibliography. Instead the acknowledgements need to be integrated into the body of the text. The reference should be given as soon as the idea has been mentioned. It is often a good idea to name the authors ('Smith says' and 'Jones argues against Smith,') and then indicate your own stand ('A more inclusive perspective, however, …'). Have a look at journal articles in your discipline to see how they refer to their sources.

Even if you formulate the ideas in your own words, you still have to furnish references. In academic papers, you need to keep mentioning authors and pages and dates to show how your ideas are related to those of the experts. It's sensible to use your own words because that saves space and lets you connect ideas smoothly. However, whether you quote a passage directly in quotation marks, paraphrase it closely in your own words, or just summarize it rapidly, you need to identify the source then and there. It is always safer to over-reference than to skimp. However, you can cut down the clutter by recognizing that some ideas are 'common knowledge' in the field—that is, taken for granted by people knowledgeable about the topic. Facts easily found in standard reference books are considered common knowledge: the dates of the Council of Ephesus, for example, or the present population of Spain. You don't need to name a specific source for them, even if you learned them only when doing your research. In some disciplines, information covered in class lectures does not need acknowledgement. Some interpretive ideas may also be so well accepted that they don't need referencing: that St Thomas Aquinas is the most distinguished medieval theologian, for instance, or that smoking is harmful to health. Check with your teacher if you are in doubt whether a specific point is considered common knowledge in your field.

The important thing is to distinguish what is your own idea from what has come from somebody else. In this enterprise, careful record-keeping is essential. Always write down the author, title and publication information (including the URL and other identifying information for web pages) so you can attach names and dates to specific ideas. Taking good notes is also essential. As you read any text—online or on the page—summarize useful points in your own words. If you record a phrase or sentence you might want to quote, put quotation marks around it *in your notes* to remind yourself that you're copying the author's exact words. Also make a deliberate effort as you read to notice connections among ideas, especially contrasts and disagreements, and also to jot down questions or thoughts of your own. If you find as you write that you're following one or two of your sources too closely, deliberately look back in your notes for other sources that take different views; then write about the differences and why they exist.

1.3.4 Organization

If you take notes efficiently, you can read with more understanding and also save time and frustration when you come to write your paper. These are three main principles involved in note taking.

First, you should know what kind of ideas you need to record. Focus your approach to the topic before you start detailed research. Then you will read with a purpose in mind, and you will be able to sort out relevant ideas. First, review the commonly known facts about your topic, and also become aware of the range of thinking and opinions on it. Review your class notes and course textbook and browse in an encyclopaedia or other reference work. Try making a preliminary list of the subtopics you would expect to find in your reading.

These will guide your attention and may come in handy as labels for notes.

Choose a component or angle that interests you, perhaps one on which there is already some controversy. Now formulate your research question. It should allow for reasoning as well as gathering of information—not just the hazards of mobile phone use in general, for instance, but how valid the current evidence is for these hazards. You may even want to jot down a tentative thesis statement as a preliminary answer to your question. Then you will know what to look for in your research reading: facts and theories that help answer your question, and other people's opinions about whether specific answers are good ones.

The second principle in taking notes is not to write down too much. Your essay or thesis must be an expression of your own thinking, not a patchwork of borrowed ideas. Plan therefore to invest your research time in understanding your sources and integrating them into your own thinking. Your note cards will record only ideas that are relevant to your focus on the topic; and they will mostly summarize rather than quote.

Copy out exact words only when the ideas are memorably phrased or surprisingly expressed—when you might use them as actual quotations in your essay. Otherwise, compress ideas in your own words. Paraphrasing word by word is a waste of time. Choose the most important ideas and write them down as labels or headings. Then fill in with a few subsidiary points that explain or exemplify the main points. Don't depend solely on underlining and highlighting. Find your own words for notes in the margin (or use sticky notes). It is necessary to label the notes intelligently. Whether you use cards or pages for note-taking, take notes in a way that allows for later use.

Save trouble later by developing the habit of recording bibliographic information in a master list when you begin looking at each source (don't forget to note book and journal information on photocopies). Then you can quickly identify each note by the author's name and page number; when you refer to sources in the essay you can fill in details of publication easily from your master list. Keep a format guide handy.

Try as far as possible to put notes on separate cards or sheets. This will let you label the topic of each note. Not only will that keep your note taking focused, but it will also allow for grouping and synthesizing of ideas later. It is especially satisfying to shuffle notes and see how the conjunctions create new ideas—yours. Leave plenty of space in your notes for comments of your own—questions and reactions as you read, second thoughts and cross-references when you look back at what you've written. These comments can become a virtual first draft of your paper.

As regards organization, it is useful to make index or note cards for collecting material. Index cards are either of the traditional, mechanical kind consisting of a series of cardboard slips which are kept in a box in alphabetical order of authors or of subjects, or else are of the electronic variety. Scholar's Aid and some of the other bibliographical software incorporate electronic note cards. Otherwise, one inexpensive electronic card system is *AZZ Cardfile* (found at www.azzcardfile.com). It incorporates many useful tools in one piece of software: it is a simple and powerful, totally customizable organizer software without predefined fields Each index 'card' is a page on a screen which then forms part of a database sorted and stored on disk. The following method is a useful one for collecting material from books, articles and manuscripts. The science of acquiring data is this way involves specifying the source in an unambiguous way, with the minimum number of parameters.

The whole text should not be copied, but rather notes are taken of the basic ideas or the expressions which are striking. If necessary, you can make photocopies or essential parts of texts studied, or else scan material directly into your computer.[9] If one scans a document, despite modern optical character recognition, the scanned text needs to be carefully checked to verify that it corresponds to the original.[10] It is unwise to put too many ideas on one card, because then it may not be easy to find the ideas again, and research will become complicated with the risk of not being able to find information when it is needed at the writing stage. At the same time, *all* the necessary information should be written down at an early stage. Much time is wasted on data lost through carelessness. It is frustrating to half-remember something which has been seen, but not copied down. Direct quotes should always be distinguished by placing them within inverted commas.

A careful distinction should be made between page numbers, folio numbers, column numbers, and article numbers. Pages are numbered on both sides (abbreviated to p. in the singular and pp. in the plural) and are most often found in books and journals. Folios are numbered

---

9. Pen-size scanners—literally about the size of a pen—are not only highly portable, but they let you scan originals like magazines and books that do not fit through a sheet feeder. The first type of scanner is used like a highlighter, scanning across the page one line at a time. The second is a pen-sized scanner that can read an entire page in a single sweep. Scanning documents in this manner requires a steady hand, as an uneven scanning rate would produce distorted images

10. Optical character recognition (usually abbreviated to OCR) is the mechanical or electronic translation of scanned images of handwritten, typewritten or printed text into machine-encoded text.

only on the front side (abbreviated to f. in the singular and ff. in the plural) and are often found in archive material. Columns are often found in patristic tomes and are numbered continuously, normally at the top of blocks into which the work is divided typographically. The abbreviation for a column is c. in the singular and cc. in the plural. Article numbers, often encountered in medieval tomes, are found in the margins alongside the division of the book in this fashion. The abbreviation is a. in the singular and aa. in the plural.

Ecclesiastical documents and legal documents are often cited according to paragraph numbers and subdivisions of paragraphs, rather than page numbers.

Examples:

> *CCEO* 66 §2 refers to paragraph 62, subsection 2 of the *Code of Canons of the Oriental Churches.*
>
> *LG* 16, refers to paragraph 16 of Vatican II, *Lumen gentium.*

It is essential to write on the index card, at the head of the notes and the copied text, all the bibliographical information, namely: the surname and initials of the author(s), the date published, the place published (which is normally a city), and the publishing house. Similarly, with an article from a journal, it is necessary to copy all the essential data, namely: the name of the journal, the volume number, and the year. Care should be taken to find out whether the pages in successive issues of the journal are numbered continuously or whether the numbering starts again with each issue. In the latter case, it is necessary to copy down the issue number (within a given year) as well as the volume number in order to specify completely where a given passage is located. The relevant page numbers must be copied down. If great care is exercised at this stage, much time will be saved later at the writing stage of the essay or thesis. Otherwise return trips to the library will be required in order to check and cross-check information which has been forgotten or omitted at this early stage of research.

Author: P. Haffner
Book Title: *Creation and Scientific Creativity*
Subtitle: *A Study in the Thought of S. L. Jaki*
Place of publication: Leominster
Publication date: 2009
Publisher: Gracewing

This work aims to be 'an introduction to Father Jaki's vast researches and profound insights on the close ties between the exact sciences and the Christian theology of Creation' (p. xii). After a brief Introduction, Chapter 1 sketches a portrait of Stanley Jaki. Chapter 2 shows how Jaki approaches science in its phenomenology and essential incompleteness; it then shows how Jaki considers the metaphysical-epistemological basis of science (pp. 42-46). Jaki's phenomenology of science underlines its pitfalls and prospects (Chapter 3); the unique rise of science in the High Middle Ages is offset against its stillbirths in all ancient cultures. This unique viable birth points to a realist metaphysics, which in turn has as its matrix the Christian doctrine of creation. Jaki's treatment of this Christian doctrine of creation as enunciated in Scripture and Tradition is examined in Chapter 4; the bond between the Christian notion of Creation and the dogma of the Incarnation is stressed. Chapter 5 deals with the adequate view of man in the Christian philosophico-theological vision, and shows how Jaki rejects materialistic and idealistic conceptions of the human person. The last three chapters of the book constitute an evaluation of Jaki's thought on the themes dealt with in the first part. Chapter 6 discusses how Jaki's critics view his discoveries concerning history and modern science. Chapter 7 then notes the crucial thrust of Jaki's thought in terms of the realist perspective. The section on Christology and cosmos makes clear what is specifically Christian in Jaki's notion of Creation. The final chapter traces the capital importance of Jaki's thought for the Church's pastoral mission today, given his creative conformity with her Magisterium.

Example: This summarizes an entire book

1.3.5 Clarity

Clarity is important to specify the purpose of the research undertaken and to know what is being sought out and where it is to be found. As a piece of written work progresses, material may well be found which will alter somewhat the direction of the work. This should not be a cause for concern; it is quite normal for research to be shaped by what is found in the course of study. Economy is one of the fundamental principles required in order to achieve clarity. Any superfluous material should be avoided, whether this be in the method, in the text or in the notes.

When you use quotations, you're letting someone else speak in the middle of your discourse. That has its uses, of course, but it also risks confusing your reader about who's speaking and what relation the quoted words have to your own argument. Student writers are often oblivious to this risk because they're not used to looking at what they've written from a reader's point of view. Rather consider the problems your reader faces. He encounters quotations used for many different purposes: to support or amplify an argument, to raise a new point, to present a point of disagreement. Don't assume your reader will understand immediately why you're using a particular quotation.

There are two main problems of clarity in using quotations. First distinguishing your own argument from the arguments of the various quoted passages; and second making sure the reader understands what a quotation is expected to accomplish.

In the first case, that of distinguishing your own argument from the argument of a quotation, sometimes you'll need to use quotations to summarize positions with which you'll disagree a little or a lot. This is especially likely to happen when you're surveying past studies or perspectives as a way of laying the groundwork for your own argument. Here's how a literary critic, Stephen Greenblatt, deals with previous approaches to Shakespeare's plays:

> Those plays have been described with impeccable intelligence as deeply conservative and with equally impeccable intelligence as deeply radical. Shakespeare, in Northrop Frye's words, is 'a born courtier,' the dramatist who organizes his representation of English history around the hegemonic mysticism of the Tudor myth; Shakespeare is also a relentless demystifier, an interrogator of ideology, 'the only dramatist,' as Franco Moretti puts it, 'who rises to the level of Machiavelli in elaborating all the consequences of the separation of political praxis from moral evaluation.' The conflict glimpsed here could be investigated, on a performance-by-performance basis.[11]

Greenblatt wishes to call attention to the 'conflict,' as he calls it, between these two views of Shakespeare (conservative or radical). He's not trying to argue that one or the other view is right, and so he crafts the passage to give each view equal weight. In the larger essay from which this excerpt is taken, Greenblatt develops his own perspective, an interpretive model that stresses 'negotiation' and ambivalence rather than imposed and settled meaning.

The other main problem of clarity that arises with quotations is to explain the reason for quoting the passage. This is especially important when the original text is ironic or carries some other non-obvious meaning. For example, the original passage below presents a quotation from Shakespeare's great villain, Iago, without doing anything to note its irony:

---

11. S. Greenblatt, *Shakespearean Negotiations: The Circulation of Social Energy in Renaissance England* (Berkeley: University of California Press, 1988), p. 23.

Original

> Iago says to Othello, 'Who steals my purse steals trash; .../.../ But he that filches from me my good name/ Robs me of that which not enriches him/ And makes me poor indeed'.[12]

Revision

> Drawing Othello further into his web, Iago suggests that public embarrassment would be intolerable: 'Who steals my purse steals trash; .../.../ But he that filches from me my good name / Robs me of that which not enriches him/ And makes me poor indeed'.[13] Iago, of course, is utterly contradicting his earlier declamation to Cassio on the folly of reputation.[14]

The revision does a much better job of helping the reader make sense of the quotation, its place in Shakespeare's play, and its function in the development of the theme of the essay.

---

12. W. Shakespeare, *Othello*, 3.3.157–161.
13. *Ibid.*.
14. *Ibid.*, 2.3.256–261.

2 THE ART OF WRITING

A good novel tells us the truth about its hero; but a bad novel tells us the truth about its author.

G. K. Chesterton, *Heretics*

Patience too is to have its practical results so that you will become fully-developed, complete, with nothing missing.

Letter of St. James 1:4

2.1 *Writing*

2.1.1 Introduction

Writing is the most creative phase of the work and depends on the personal contribution of each student. Some basic guidelines should be followed in the elaboration of the text. It must not simply be a piece of patchwork, in which various interesting texts are sewn together with a bit of personal reflection. Rather it should be a synthetic expression of personal thought. You are not writing only because you have to write something, but because you have something to write. For this reason, care must be taken to avoid too many citations from authors. Quotations are meant to illustrate what you are saying, and should be like seasoning in food. Generally, quotations should not make up much more than 10% of the text. At some points in the text, more quotation may be necessary. At other points, like the introduction and conclusion, fewer, if any, citations will be needed.

2.1.2 The plan

A plan should be employed to ensure that one part flows logically into the next one so that the whole fits together in a coherent way. It is pertinent to remember what St Thomas Aquinas said: 'Beauty includes three conditions, integrity or perfection; due proportion or harmony; and lastly, brightness, or clarity.'[1] Thus, the thought should proceed logically and in an ordered fashion within each section. The discussion has to be unfolded with discipline. Unlike writing a book where there is more freedom, working on an essay or a thesis makes greater demands on formality. Sometimes it is necessary to move material from one chapter to another where it fits better. This process is rather like trying on clothes for size. References with their footnotes or end notes are made according to the directives given below in chapter five.

If English is not the first language of the writer of the essay or thesis, the student should have someone whose first language is English to correct the text before it is finally presented. Lecturers or professors (even from other universities) should not be asked to correct English, because that is not their job, and also it introduces a possibility that they may help the candidate unduly in the formulation of the text. Rather the help should come from a friend or colleague, or else a professional corrector.

Each paragraph should generally contain one main idea and should be neither too short nor too long. Each page should normally contain about two or three paragraphs. The main idea should be introduced at the beginning of the paragraph. Make the paragraph the unit of composition: one paragraph should be assigned to each topic. If the subject on which you are writing is of

1. St Thomas Aquinas, *Summa Theologiae* I, q.39, a.8.

small extent, or if you intend to treat it very briefly, there may be no need to subdivide it into topics. Thus with a brief description, a brief summary of a literary work, a brief account of a single incident, a narrative merely outlining an action, the setting forth of a single idea, any one of these is best written in a single paragraph. After the paragraph has been written, it should be examined to see whether subdivision will improve it. Ordinarily, a subject requires subdivision into topics, each of which should be made the subject of a paragraph. The object of treating each topic in a paragraph by itself is to aid the reader. The beginning of each paragraph is a signal to him that a new step in the development of the subject has been reached.

As a rule, begin each paragraph with a sentence (the topic sentence) outlining the idea you wish to convey; end it in conformity with the beginning. Again, the object is to aid the reader. The practice recommended here enables him to discover the purpose of each paragraph as he begins to read it, and to retain the purpose in mind as he ends it. For this reason, the most generally useful kind of paragraph, particularly in exposition and argument, is that in which the topic sentence comes at or near the beginning; the succeeding sentences explain or establish or develop the statement made in the topic sentence; and the final sentence either emphasizes the thought of the topic sentence or states some important consequence.

Ending with a digression, or with an unimportant detail, is particularly to be avoided. If the paragraph forms part of a larger composition, its relation to what precedes, or its function as a part of the whole, may need to be expressed. This can sometimes be done by a mere word or phrase (*again; therefore; for the same reason*) in the topic sentence. Sometimes, however, it is expedient to precede the topic sentence by one or more sentences of introduction or transition. If more than one such sentence is required, it is generally better to set apart the transitional sentences as a separate paragraph.

According to your purpose, you may relate the body of the paragraph to the topic sentence in one or more of several different ways. You may make the meaning of the topic sentence clearer by restating it in other forms, by defining its terms, by denying the converse, by giving illustrations or specific instances; you may establish it by proofs; or you may develop it by showing its implications and consequences. In a long paragraph, you may adopt several of these processes.

2.2 Consistency and coherence

Consistency and coherence are very important in any piece of academic written work. Now several examples will be offered of where consistency and coherence come into play. We will start with the larger components of a written piece and proceed to the smaller ones.

2.2.1 Paragraphs and headings

Every new paragraph is consistently indented a fixed amount (usually between 0.5 and 1 cm). In British style, the first paragraph of a chapter or a section is not indented, but all the subsequent paragraphs are indented. After a block quote, an example or a list, the first normal paragraph is not indented, but all the subsequent paragraphs are indented.

The way in which block quotes are constructed, with a specific font size, and right and left indentation, should be consistent throughout the work.[2] Similarly, headings

2. See chapter five, subsection 5.2.1, where we remark that a quotation longer than five lines is put in an indented single-spaced section on its own, without quotation marks, in a style known as a block quote.

and subheadings should be made with consistently sized and styled fonts (bold or italic or both) and consistent spacings from the text body.

2.2.2 *British or American usage*

A decision should be made at the start of the work either to adopt British or American usage; this will govern spellings of words like colour or color. It will also require attention regarding verbs ending in -ize or -ise and their derivatives, the forms in -ize, -ization, (like civilize, civilization or civilise, civilisation).

English spelling	*American Spelling*
recognise	recognize (sometimes English too)
behaviour	behavior
recognising	recognizing (sometimes English too)
paralyse	paralyze
generalisations	generalizations (sometimes English too)
labelling	labeling
analyse	analyze
programme	program
hypoglycaemia	hypoglycemia
travelling	traveling
revitalise	revitalize (sometimes English too)
practise (the verb)	practice (Am. both verb and noun!)
apologising	apologizing (sometimes English too)
defence	defense
channelled	chanelled
finalised	finalized (sometimes English too)

Some words, because of their origin, must, however, have the -ise spelling, such as:

advertise, comprise, devise, franchise, revise, advise, compromise, enterprise, improvise, supervise, apprise, demise, excise, incise, surmise, chastise, despise, exercise, premise, surprise.

A special case occurs with words connected with the expression 'fulfil'. Here very special care must be exercised in order to achieve consistency.

English spelling	*American Spelling*
fulfil	fulfill
fulfilling	fulfiling
fulfilment	fulfillment
fulfiller	fulfiler

Note that 'billion' means 'a million million' in UK English, but 'a thousand million' in US English.

Another difference between British and American English lies in the use of quotation marks. In American English, the most basic rule of single and double quotation marks is simply that double quotation marks should be used by default for enclosing quotations. Single quotation marks (or inverted commas), on the other hand, are employed for enclosing quotations that exist within quotations. In British English, at least in standard usage for published books, this rule is inverted, with the default mode being the inverted comma, and double quotation marks being used only for quotes within quotes. Over time, however, this praxis has gradually shifted, and it is now not uncommon to see many followers of British English begin with double quotation marks. In this book, we have adhered to the British style both in the body of the work, and in the examples. We acknowledge that in student usage for papers and theses, even in British usage, the default mode may often be double quotation marks for quotes, and inverted commas for quotes within quotes. Thus the student may need to adapt the examples furnished in this manual to comply with his or her preference and that of the academic institution in question.

2.2.3 *References and bibliographies*

A consistent method should be employed for making references (of which more will be said in chapter five) and constructing bibliographies (of which more in chapter six).

2.2.4 *Abbreviations*

Abbreviations should be made in a consistent manner, preferably with the aid of a table as indicated in chapter three, subsection 3.2.2, below.

2.2.5 *Singular and plural*

Some nouns borrowed from foreign languages carry only the straightforward English plural, like:[3]

> (Greek) acropolis, acropolises.
>
> (Latin) campus, campuses; census, censuses; octopus, octopuses; album, albums; forum, forums; museum, museums; premium, premiums.
>
> (Italian) canto, cantos; libretto, librettos; soprano, sopranos; sonata, sonatas; opera, operas.

Other nouns, especially ones adopted from Greek and Latin, take only the foreign plural ending, like:

> (Greek) analysis, analyses; axis, axes; basis, bases; crisis, crises; diagnosis, diagnoses; oasis, oases; thesis, theses (analogously with hypothesis, parenthesis, synthesis); criterion, criteria; phenomenon, phenomena.

---

3. Many of these examples are taken from *MHRA Style Guide: A Handbook for Authors, Editors, and Writers of Theses* (London: Modern Humanities Research Association, 2008), 2.7.

(Latin) alumnus, alumni; cactus, cacti; addendum, addenda; datum, data; desideratum, desiderata; erratum, errata; codex, codices.

(German) lied, lieder.

Other borrowed nouns may carry either the English or the foreign plural. In general, the foreign plural is less common and more formal, or it may have a more specialized sense, as in these words of Greek or Latin origin:

formula (formulas in everyday usage, formulae in mathematics); thesaurus (thesauruses, thesauri); medium (mediums in spiritualism, media for (plural) means of communication); memorandum (memorandums, memoranda); referendum (referendums, referenda); ultimatum (ultimatums, ultimata); corpus (corpuses, corpora); appendix (appendixes for parts of the body, appendixes or appendices for additional parts of a publication); index (indexes for alphabetical lists of references, indices in mathematics).

Some adopted French words may retain the original plural -x, but the plural -s is also found:

adieu (adieus, adieux); milieu (milieus, milieux); tableau (tableaus, tableaux).

No apostrophe should be used before the plural ending of abbreviations (where the -s follows any punctuation), names, numbers, letters, and words not normally used as nouns, like the following:

The 1890s in Europe are widely regarded as years of social decadence.

Rosa and her brother have identical IQs, and they both have PhDs from Harvard.

Nevertheless, care needs to be taken, because the Welsh plural of Jones is Joneses.

Keeping up with the Joneses
and not Keeping up with the Jones' (nor with the Jones's).

2.2.6 Upper case and lower case

Our first example lies in the use of upper case and lower case. Either one or the other must be used consistently throughout the work. For example if 'Him' is used for God, then this must be done all the way through, with all other personal pronouns.

1. Thus 'You' must be used for God instead of 'you'. Upper case must also be used for personal pronouns referring to Jesus Christ. It is incorrect and unacceptable to use upper case for personal pronouns referring to God and lower case for those referring to Jesus Christ. Upper case is employed for Our Blessed Lady. The choice of upper case also implies that, for example, Creation (the divine action), Incarnation, Resurrection, Ascension and Second Coming all commence with capital letters.
2. Original sin need not be in upper case, however the Fall should be capitalized to indicate that it is not just any fall!
3. Specific organizations and groups also take a capital letter, while general references do not. Thus, the East India Company, but a company.
4. Geographical locations carry an initial capital when they are recognized regions. Thus, the Arun Valley, but the north-west.
5. Historical periods of time are lower case is used in a general sense (e.g. medieval manuscripts) but upper case if they refer to a specific historical period (e.g. Roman remains, the High Middle Ages). A church building in general is specified in lower case, while a particular edifice is in upper case, like St. James' Church.
6. Religious bodies carry an initial capital letter, where the reference is to an institution, for example Catholic, Catholicism, the Catholic Church. The necessary

distinction between the particular church (or local church) and the Universal Church is conveyed by the use of lower and upper case respectively.

7. When ecclesiastical and noble forms are attached to the full title, they should always carry an initial capital letter. Thus, one should write Pope Urban VIII, the Queen of England, the Cardinal Archbishop of Westminster, the Duke of Kent. The same holds on other occasions when the titles are specific, such as the Pope, the Queen, the Cardinal, referring to a particular person. When the titles are general, they are in lower case, such as a queen, a cardinal, a duke. However, some publishing houses would put a Pope in upper case even in general. A similar principle can be applied to councils. In general terms, an ecumenical council would be in lower case, but a specific instance like the Second Vatican Council would be in upper case. Local councils follow the same principle, like the 11th Council of Toledo.
8. The names of movements or styles usually take upper case when derived from proper nouns (such as Aristotelian, Thomistic, Romanesque) but otherwise begin in lower case (like baroque, imperialism, modernism).

2.2.7 Italics

Avoid the use of italics for rhetorical emphasis. Any word or phrase individually discussed should, however, be in italics, and any interpretation of it in single quotation marks.

Example:

> C. S. Lewis defined *agape* as 'a selfless love, a love that was passionately committed to the well-being of the other'.

In this example, *agape* is italicized both because it is a Greek word, and also because it is being defined. It may also be desirable to use italics to distinguish one word or phrase from another. If you are in doubt about whether to italicize a word, type it as though it were not italic and see what effect that makes. Single words or short phrases in foreign languages not used as direct quotations should be in italics. Direct, acknowledged, or more substantial quotations should be in normal type, within inverted commas.

Foreign words and phrases which have passed into regular English usage should not be italicized, though the decision between italic and normal type may sometimes be a fine one. In doubtful instances it is usually best to use normal.

The following are examples of words which are no longer italicized:[4]

> avant-garde, dilettante, milieu, role,
> cliché, ennui, par excellence, salon,
> debris, genre, per cent, status quo,
> denouement, leitmotif, résumé, vice versa.

Certain Latin words and abbreviations which are in common English usage are also no longer italicized. For example:

> cf., e.g., et al., etc., ibid., i.e., passim, viz.

Exceptions are made of the Latin *sic*, frequently used within quotations and therefore conveniently differentiated by the use of italic, and of *circa* (abbreviated as *c*.). Names of institutions or organizations abroad are written in normal letters with initial capitals, like 'Pontificia Università Gregoriana'.

The titles of works published independently (not within another volume) are typically formatted with italics. These include books, plays, long poems published

4. This is the considered opinion of the *MHRA Style Guide*, 7.2.

as books, pamphlets, newspapers, magazines, journals, films, radio and television programs, web sites, CDs, DVDs, software, ballets, operas, paintings, and other works and artefacts that stand on their own. In the biological and medical sciences, genera and species should be italicised, but not family:

> *Gossypium herbaceum* is short-fibre cotton, while *Gossypium barbadense* has relatively long fibres.
>
> The genus *Anopheles* belongs to the mosquito family or Culicidae.

The titles of works published within larger works should be in normal type enclosed within single quotation marks. These include articles, essays, stories, short poems, chapters, encyclopedia entries, sections of online documents, songs, and individual episodes of broadcast programmes. The titles of poems, short stories, or essays which form part of a larger volume or other whole, or the first lines of poems used as titles, should also be given in normal type in single quotation marks:[5]

> Thomas Edward Brown's 'My Garden';
> Browning's 'Song from "Paracelsus"';
> Burns's 'A Red, Red Rose';
> Emily Brontë's 'Remembrance';
> Robert Hugh Benson's 'At High Mass'.

The titles of collections of manuscripts should be given in normal type without quotation marks. The titles of published or unpublished theses should be given in italic type. Titles of other works which appear within an

5. Note the use of double quotation marks for a quotation within a quotation, in the second example. This is common British usage for published books. However, I acknowledge that many students adopt double quotation marks for the main quotation and single marks within the quotation. The usage in the USA is also for double quotation marks, and single marks within.

italicized title should be printed in normal without any quotation marks:

> *An Approach to* Macbeth.

In the citation of legal cases the names of the contending parties are given in italics, but the intervening 'v.' (for 'versus') is in normal:

> *Bardell* v. *Pickwick.*

Titles of films, substantial musical compositions, and works of art are italicized:[6]

> *When in Rome*; *Charles VI*; *Amahl and the Night Visitors*; Beethoven's *Eroica* Symphony; *The Martyrdom of Saint Agatha*; *Die schöne Müllerin*; *The Spy Next Door*; *The Haywain*; *The Last Judgement*; Taverner's *Missa Sancti Wilhelmi.*

Descriptive or numerical titles such as the following, however, take neither italics nor quotation marks:[7]

> Beethoven's Third Symphony; Bach's Mass in B minor; Mendelssohn's Andante and Scherzo; Piano Concerto No. 1 in B flat minor.

If a proper name is part of the symphony then that name can carry italics:

> Mozart's *Haffner* Symphony.

Titles of songs and other short individual pieces (like those of poems) are given in normal and within single quotation marks:[8]

> 'Light of the World'; 'Roma, alma parens'; 'Mercury, the Winged Messenger' from Holst's *The Planets.*

Special rules apply to punctuation with italics.[9] There are italic forms of most punctuation marks. The type

6. See *MHRA Style Guide*, 7.4.
7. *Ibid.*.
8. *Ibid.*.
9. See *ibid.*, 5.5.

style (normal or italics) of the main part of any sentence will govern the style of the punctuation marks within or concluding it. If the main part of a sentence is in normal but an italic word within it immediately precedes a punctuation mark, that mark will normally be in normal. However, if the punctuation mark occurs within a phrase or title which is entirely in italics, or if the punctuation mark belongs to the phrase in italics rather than to the sentence as a whole, the punctuation mark will be in italics:[10]

> Where is a crime more brilliantly portrayed than in Agatha Christie's *4.50 from Paddington*?
>
> *The Floating Admiral* is a collaborative detective novel written by fourteen members of the Detection Club in 1931.
>
> Dorothy Sayers penned *Creed or Chaos?: Why Christians Must Choose Either Dogma or Disaster*.
>
> Who was the author of *Why Didn't They Ask Evans?*?

Affairs get more complicated when you have titles within italicised titles. Here I propose substituting normal for italics in titles within italicized titles like:

> *Understanding* At Bertram's Hotel: *Critical Readings*.
>
> *A Key to Whitehead's* Process and Reality.

This avoids using quotation marks which do not figure in the original.[11]

2.2.8 Personal names

Where generally accepted English forms of classical names exist (Horace, Livy, Ptolemy, Virgil), they should be adopted. Names of Popes and saints should normally be given in their English form (Gregory, Innocent, Paul, St Thomas Aquinas, St John of the Cross, St Francis of

10. See *ibid.*.

11. Here I beg to differ from the *MHRA Style Guide*, 5.5.

Assisi). Names of foreign kings and queens should normally be given in their English form where one exists (Charles V, Catherine the Great, Ferdinand and Isabella, Francis I, Henry IV, Victor Emmanuel). Those names for which no English form exists (Haakon, Sancho) or for which the English form is quaint or archaic (Alphonse, Lewis for Alfonso, Louis) should retain their foreign form. If in the course of a work it is necessary to refer to some monarchs whose names have acceptable English forms and some which do not, in the interests of consistency it is better to use the foreign form for all:[12]

> The reigns of Fernando III and Alfonso X.
>
> Henri IV was succeeded by Louis XIII.

Care must be taken over the spelling of names involving Mc, Mac, and similar particles (like McDonald, MacDonald, Macmillan, Mac Liammóir); one should adopt the form used by the individual in question. All these forms are alphabetized taking into account the exact spelling of the particle.[13] Likewise, it is necessary to distinguish between Irish names that retain their original form (Ó Máille) and those that are anglicized (O'Donnell). The Irish girl's name Siobhan is rarely anglicised to Chivorne. Welsh names involving ap, ab (son of) or ferch (daughter of) are neither capitalized nor hyphenated.[14] Names of historical figures are alphabetized under the first name (e.g. Dafydd ap Gwilym, Dafydd ab Owain), while modern names under ap or ab (e.g. ap Gwilym, ab Owen Edwards).

---

12. See *MHRA Style Guide*, 3.3.2.1.
13. Here I beg to differ from the recommendation of the *MHRA Style Guide*, 3.3.1. See also chapter six below, subsection 6.1.1 C.
14. See J. Davies, N. Jenkins, M. Baines and P. I. Lynch, *The Welsh Academy Encyclopedia of Wales* (Cardiff: University of Wales Press, 2008).

Various systems exist for the transliteration of Russian and other languages using the Cyrillic alphabet.[15] If one is working in the field of Slavonic studies, one should ascertain which system is preferred and conform to it strictly. Russian and other Slavonic names referred to in other contexts should, wherever possible, be given in the form recommended by *The New Oxford Dictionary for Writers and Editors*, even when this conflicts with the Library of Congress system: Dostoevsky, Shostakovich, Tolstoy, Yevtushenko.[16] Note in particular that, except in the one case of Tchaikovsky, Ch- not Tch should be used (e.g. Chekhov) and that the prime (′) should not be used: Gogol, Gorky, Ilya (compare Library of Congress: Gogol′, Gor′ kii, Il′ ia).

Take care with consistency in the capitalization or otherwise of particles in foreign names (like Philippe Du Puy de Clinchamps, Vasco da Gama, Jan Van der Vliedt).[17] Do not abbreviate 'Saint' and 'Sainte' in French surnames:

> Françoise de Saint-Clair (not Françoise de St.-Clair).

Hyphenated Asian names do not take a full-stop after the first initial:

> Jen-Yi Hwang is J-Y. Hwang not J.-Y. Hwang.

Note how this differs from the abbreviation of Jean-Marc Lafayette, which is J.-M. Lafayette.

---

15. Tradition holds that Cyrillic was developed by Saints Cyril and Methodius who brought Christianity to the southern Slavs.

16. See *The New Oxford Dictionary for Writers and Editors* (Oxford: Oxford University Press, 2005).

17. We will have more to say about particles in chapter six on bibliography, subsection 6.1.1.

2.2.9 *Place names*

If there is a current English form for non-English place names (Florence, Havana, Lampeter, Lisbon, Majorca, Moscow, Munich, Naples, Padua, Rheims, Salonika, Venice, Vienna, and so forth), it can be used. However, obsolete English forms (like Carnarvon, Francfort, Leipsic, Leghorn) should be avoided. The forms Luxembourg and Strasbourg have now largely superseded Luxemburg and Strasburg or Strassburg and are therefore recommended. One should be consistent within a given work about the use of English forms like Lyons and Marseilles or the French forms (Lyon, Marseille).

The use or non-use of hyphens in names such as Newcastle upon Tyne, Stratford-upon-Avon should be checked in a reliable reference work. French place names are regularly hyphenated, like Colombey-les-Deux-Églises, Châlons-sur-Marne, Saint-Malo. Where there is an introductory definite article, (as in the cases of Le Havre, Les Baux-de-Provence), the article is not hyphenated to the rest of the place name.[18]

The definite article is no longer used in the names of the countries Lebanon, Sudan and Ukraine, but it is employed for the Gambia, and the Netherlands.

2.2.10 *Punctuation*

Concerning quotations and punctuation, care should be exercised to be correct and consistent. A *comma* within a quoted text generally falls inside the quotation marks because it is part of the text, thus:

> 'The ultimate synthesis,' Jaki notes, 'the rock-bottom layer of the material world, is today as far away as it has ever been.'

---

18. See *MHRA Style Guide*, 3.1.

The *full-stop* should also generally be put within the quotation marks as in the example above. However, many publications use a more refined approach, based on the so-called Hart's Rules. These rules regulate that punctuation which *actually belongs to the cited text* falls inside the quotation marks, while the other punctuation should remain outside. These rules indicate that where a full sentence, with an initial capital letter, is quoted at the end of the sentence, the full-stop precedes the inverted commas. In all other instances, when only a phrase is quoted, the full-stop should follow the inverted commas. Other punctuation marks are placed in relation to quotation marks according to sense.

Examples:

1) He said: 'It is an excellent idea.'

2) He said it was 'an excellent idea'.

3) 'It is', he said, 'an excellent idea.'

4) 'It is,' he said, 'for the most part, an excellent idea.'

If a short quotation is used at the end of a sentence, the final full-stop should be outside the closing quotation mark:

> Do not be afraid of what Stevenson calls 'a little judicious levity'.

This rule applies even when a quotation ends with a full-stop in the original, and when a quotation forms a complete sentence in the original but, as quoted, is integrated within a sentence of introduction or comment without intervening punctuation:

> We learn at once that 'Miss Brooke had that kind of beauty which seems to be thrown into relief by poor dress'.

For quotations which are either interrogatory or exclamatory, punctuation marks should appear both before and after the closing quotation mark:

> The pause is followed by Richard's demanding 'will no man say "Amen"?'.

> Why does Shakespeare give Malcolm the banal question 'Oh, by whom?'?

The final full-stop should precede the closing quotation mark only when the quotation forms a complete sentence and is separated from the preceding passage by a punctuation mark. Such a quotation may be interrupted:

> Wilde said, 'He found in stones the sermons he had already hidden there.'

> Soames added: 'Well, I hope you both enjoy yourselves.'

> Hardy's *Satires of Circumstance* was not well received. 'The gloom', wrote Lytton Strachey in his review of it, 'is not even relieved by a little elegance of diction.'

In this last example, the comma after 'gloom' follows the quotation mark as there is no comma in the original. Contrast:

> 'It is a far, far better thing that I do,' Carton asserts, 'than I have ever done.'

Here the original has a comma after 'I do'. But when the quotation ends in a question mark or an exclamation mark, it is not followed by a comma:

> 'What think you of books?' said he.

When a short quotation is followed by a reference in parentheses, the final punctuation should follow the closing parenthesis:

> He assumes the effect to be 'quite deliberate' (p. 29).

> There is no reason to doubt the effect of this 'secret humiliation' (Book 6, Chapter 52).

2.2.11 *The possessive*

The possessive of proper names ending in a pronounced -s or other sibilant is normally formed by adding an apostrophe and s:[19]

> Alvarez's criticism, Berlioz's symphonies, Cervantes's works, Dickens's characters, in Inigo Jones's day, Keats's poems, Rubens's paintings.

However, the possessive of Moses and of Greek names ending in -es (particularly those having more than two syllables) is frequently formed by means of an apostrophe alone:[20]

> under Moses' leadership, Demosthenes' speeches,
> Sophocles' plays, Xerxes' campaigns.

The possessive of names ending in -us conforms to the normal rule:

> Claudius's successor, Herodotus's Histories,
> Jesus's parables, an empire greater than Darius's

Note that French names ending in an unpronounced -s, -x, or -z follow the normal rule and take an apostrophe and s:[21]

> Rabelais's comedy, Descartes's works,
> Malraux's style, Cherbuliez's novels

2.2.12 *Diacritics*

These are marks attached to *letters* of the alphabet that show (i) how the pronunciation differs from that of the

---

19. See *ibid.*, 2.5.2.

20. See *ibid.*.

21. See *ibid.*.

unmarked letter, (ii) where the stress falls in a polysyllabic word or (iii) what tone or pitch goes with a particular word.

When citing German words, use ß (eszett) for ss, but only in lower case (and note that not all ss are ß); in capitals (and small capitals), SS is always used. Use umlauts over ä, ö and ü rather than using the respective diphthongs ae, oe and ue. Remember that, in German, all nouns have initial capitals (e.g. ein Haus, das Sein) and they should retain these when italicized.

In French Upper-case letters carry accents, like:

RÉSUMÉ

The exception is the preposition *à:*

A la porte.

Scandinavian characters should be alphabetized as follows:

Z, Æ, Ø, Å (Danish, Norwegian)

Z, Þ, Æ, Ö (Icelandic)

Z, Å, Ä, Ö (Finnish, Swedish)

There is often inconsistency between dictionaries (and sometimes within the same dictionary) as to the use of accents and other diacritics on words borrowed from other languages.

Two cases are fairly clear:

(i) When a word or, more often, an expression is still felt to be foreign (and an objective decision is not always possible), all diacritics should be retained, like:

aide-mémoire, ancien régime, à la mode, Aufklärung, la belle époque, bête noire, cause célèbre, déjà vu, éminence grise, Führer, lycée, maître d'hôtel, papier mâché, pièce de résistance, raison d'être, señor, succès de scandale, tête-à-tête.

Such words and expressions are often also italicized.
(ii) Words ending in -é retain their accent: blasé, café, cliché, exposé, fiancé (also fiancée) In such words, any other accents are also retained, for example:[22]

> émigré, pâté, protégé, résumé.

However, in the case of some words that have passed into regular English usage, diacritics are often dropped, as in the following:[23]

> chateau, crepe, debacle, debris, denouement, detente, echelon, elite, fete, hotel, matinee, premiere, regime, role, soiree.

Nevertheless in other words, the accents are maintained:

> crèche, décor, crêpes Suzette, naïve, précis, séance.

The important rule is to be consistent throughout your work with the way that a given word is accented,

2.2.13 Dashes

There are three types of dashes in current use: The hyphen, the En Dash, and the Em Dash. Here we will see how to use them all correctly.

a) Hyphen (-)

The hyphen is the minus key in Windows-based keyboards. This is a widely used punctuation mark, and should not be mistaken for a dash. The dash is different and has different function than a hyphen.

In formal essays, it is usually best to avoid splitting words too often at the end of a line. If you must, be sure to put the hyphen after a complete syllable: splut-ter; sesqui-pedalian. Most word-processors and desktop publishing programs include automatic hyphenation; if

---

22. See *ibid.*, 2.2

23. This is the recommendation of the *MHRA Style Guide*, 2.2.

you use it, check where the words are split, since the program's algorithm, however sophisticated, will not always put the hyphen where a human would. Also, do not hyphenate an already hyphenated word (e.g. anti-es-tablishment).

A hyphen is used to separate the words in a compound adjective, verb, or adverb. For instance:

The T-rex has a movement-based vision.
My blog is blogger-powered.
John's idea was pooh-poohed.

The hyphen can be used generally for all kinds of word-breaks. However, hyphens should be used only when they have a specific purpose. They may serve to separate the parts of a complex word so as to avoid awkward sequences of letters (e.g., re-enter, co-opt) but they normally indicate that two or more words are to be read as a single word with only one main stress. The examples given below show forms that are attributive and have a single main stress and are therefore hyphenated, while predicative and other forms having two main stresses are not hyphenated:

a well-known fact
the facts are well known

a tenth-century manuscript
in the tenth century

a late-eighteenth-century novelist
written in the late eighteenth century.

In phrases such as 'pre- and post-war governments', 'eighteenth- and nineteenth-century literature', where two or more parallel hyphenated terms are combined, a hyphen is left hanging, that is, it is followed by a space. Adverbs ending in -ly are not hyphenated to a following adjective or participle:[24]

---

24. See *MHRA Style Guide*, 2.3.

a highly contentious argument
a recently published novel
a handsomely bound volume
a frequently occurring mistake.

Collocations of certain monosyllabic adverbs (in particular ill but not well—see above) and a participle often have only one main stress and are therefore hyphenated even when used predicatively:

He is very ill-disposed.
Such a course of action would be ill-advised.

Note that, unlike the words early, late, north, south, and so forth, the prefix mid- always requires a hyphen (except where it forms part of a single word, as in midnight):[25]

The boat sank in mid-Atlantic
a mid-June midnight flight
a mid-sixteenth-century chair
until the mid-nineteenth century.

The presence or absence of a hyphen is often significant:[26]

'two-year-old rabbits' but 'two year-old rabbits'
'a deep-blue lake' but 'a deep blue lake'
'a vice-chancellor' but 'the vice squad'
'to re-cover' but 'to recover'.

Usage shifts over time and forms that were once entirely acceptable may now seem odd or old-fashioned. Some words that used to be hyphenated have now become so common that they are regarded as single unhyphenated words: battlefield, bookshelf, paperback, subcommittee, subtitle. In short, if a compound is in frequent use and is pronounced as a single word it is usually acceptable to write it as one word without a hyphen. There is considerable variation in the use of hyphens and it is almost impossible to formulate comprehensive rules. The best

25. See *ibid.*.

26. See *ibid.*.

advice is to use a good dictionary or spell checker and to be consistent.

b) En Dash (–)

The En Dash derives its name from its width. It is one 'N' long (En is a typographical unit that is almost as wide as 'N'). The En Dash is used to express a range of values or a distance:

> People of age 55–80 are more prone to hypertension.
> The Delhi–Sidney flight was late by three hours.

In expressing game scores, the En Dash is used.

> India beat Pakistan 250–190.

Use the En Dash in compound adjectives in which the two participant terms themselves are compound.

> Hyper-threaded–land-grid-array processor powers my PC.

The En Dash is also to express page ranges like pp. 45–78.

c) Em Dash (—)

The Em Dash derives its name from its width, which is roughly one 'M' long or two 'N' long (Em is a typographical unit twice the length of en—and almost the length of capital 'M'). The Em Dash is used to set off parenthetical elements, which are abrupt. This is different from commas separating parenthetical elements. For instance:

> The tea—with cardamom and other spices—was delicious and fragrant.

The Em Dash also separates the final part of a sentence that is logically not part of the sentence (similar to the colon use in this context).

> Several friends were present—Jane, John, and Laura, among them.

Though most people prefer to follow the Em Dash without spaces, some people recommend using Em dash or En Dash with spaces around. Always keep an eye on these elements of punctuation when you edit your work. Avoiding mistakes in writing is extremely important for getting published; being careful to avoid even the slightest mistake makes a writer great.

2.2.14 Parentheses and Brackets

In the strict sense, the term 'brackets' means 'square brackets', like [ ], and should not be confused with parentheses, like ( ). However, since the term is widely misused, it is as well always to specify square brackets, round brackets (or parentheses), angle brackets, like < >, or braces, like { }.[27]

Parentheses are used for parenthetical statements and references within a text, if you are using parenthetic methods of making references.[28] Remember to leave a space outside but not inside the parentheses. When a passage within parentheses falls at the end of a sentence of which it is only a part, the final full-stop is placed outside the closing parenthesis:[29]

> She finally passed her driving test (after three unsuccessful attempts).

Parentheses are also used to add the technical name of a species:

> The Japanese wineberry (*Rubus phoenicolasius*) produces small, red fruits on extremely bristly, red stems.

When a complete sentence is within parentheses, the final full-stop should be inside the closing parenthesis. Parentheses may be used within parentheses:

---

27. See *ibid.*, 5.3.
28. See chapter five, section 5.6 for more about this topic.
29. See *MHRA Style Guide*, 5.3.

(His presidential address (1987) made this point clearly.)

Square brackets should be used for the enclosure of phrases or words which have been added to the original text or for editorial and similar comments:[30]

> He adds that 'the lady [Mrs Smith] had suffered great misfortunes'.
>
> I do not think they should have [two words illegible].
>
> He swore to tell the truth, the old [sic] truth, and nothing but the truth.

2.2.15 *Ellipsis*

An ellipsis (…) is used to mark the omission of a word or phrase in a quoted passage. Four ellipsis points (actually a period plus three ellipsis points) mark an omission between sentences. In a quotation of several paragraphs, the omission of an intervening paragraph (or paragraphs) is indicated by a period plus three ellipsis points at the end of the paragraph preceding the omitted parts. And if a paragraph other than the first one begins with a sentence that does not open the paragraph, it should be preceded by three ellipsis points plus the usual paragraph indentation.
Ellipses should not be used

1. before or after an obviously incomplete sentence;
2. before a block quotation beginning with a complete sentence or an incomplete sentence that completes a sentence in the text;
3. after a block quotation that ends with a complete sentence;
4. before or after a run-in quotation of a complete sentence.

---

30. See *ibid.*.

Examples:

'Christ ... fulfils this prophetic office, not only by the hierarchy ... but also by the laity.'

'The most important member is Christ, since He is the Head.... Therefore the riches of Christ are communicated to all the members.'

2.2.16 *Early forms*

The spelling of quotations is generally always that of the book or edition referred to. However, in quotations from early printed books the forms of the letters i and j, u and v, w, the long s (ſ or ʃ), the ampersand (&), the Tironian sign (7), the tilde, superior letters in contractions, and other abbreviations are regularized to accord with modern usage. If there are good reasons to the contrary, like, for example, in full bibliographical descriptions, the ancient form is then adopted.[31]

2.2.17 *Numbers*

a) Dates and times

A consistent choice should be made between 15 September 1993 (often the English usage) and September 15, 1993 (usually the American form). In particular it is preferable to adopt '15' for the day and not '15th'. No internal punctuation should be employed except when a day of the week is mentioned, like 'Friday, 12 October 2001'. If it is necessary to refer to a date in both Old and New Calendars, the form '11/21 July 1605' should be used. For dates dependent upon the time of beginning the new year the form '21 January 1564/5' should

31. For more on this topic, see M. Bland, *A Guide to Early Printed Books and Manuscripts* (Chichester: John Wiley, 2010).

be adopted. When referring to a period of time use the form 'from 1826 to 1850' (not 'from 1826–50'), 'from January to March 1970' (not 'from January–March 1970'). In citations of the era, 'BC' (before Christ), 'BCE' (before the Christian era, before the common era), and 'CE' (Christian era, common era) follow the year and 'AD' (Anno Domini) precedes it, and small capitals without full-stops are employed:[32]

> 83 BC, 83 BCE, 367 CE, AD 367

With reference to centuries, all of these abbreviations, including 'AD', follow:

> in the fifth century AD

In references to decades, an 's' without an apostrophe should be adopted:[33]

> the 1960s (not the 1960's, nor the 60's)

In references to centuries the ordinal should be spelled out, and not left as a figure:

> In the sixth century it reached its peak; by the twentieth it was over.

Where century numbers are used as an adjective, they require a hyphen:

> In sixth-century graves
> In late twelfth-century Ireland
> In mid-eighteenth-century France

Note the second hyphen after 'mid' in the last example. When citing approximate dates, *circa* should be abbreviated as c.:

---

32. See *MHRA Style Guide*, 8.1. Common era notation is open to the criticism that it is the result of an attempt to exclude explicit Christian influence within society, and therefore a result of secularization, religious syncretism or political correctness.

33. See *ibid.*.

c. 1480, c. 400 BC

In text, spell out the time of day unless you are referring to a precise time.

Committee meetings never end before five.

Her parents insisted that she be home by midnight at the weekend.

The bus leaves Emsworth at 6:45 each evening.

Vatican radio will air the interview tomorrow morning at 8:30.

Always use figures with a.m. and p.m. Never use morning with a.m., or evening with p.m., and never use o'clock with a.m. or p.m.

8 a.m., 12 p.m. (noon), 4:30 in the morning, 12 a.m. (midnight), 9:45 p.m., 6 o'clock

In text, do not use zeros with even hours, except for consistency within a series:

Ottawa will return to standard time at 2 a.m. Sunday.

Morning classes were scheduled for 8:30, 10:00, and 11:30.

Be consistent in your use of the twelve hour or the twenty-four hour clock.

b) Numerals

Numbers up to one hundred, including ordinals, should be written in words when the context is not statistical. Figures should be used for volume, part, chapter, and page numbers; but note this usage:

The third chapter is longer than the fourth.

Figures are also used for years, including those below one hundred. However, numbers at the beginning of sentences and approximate numbers should be expressed in words. Also, when referring to a round quantity (hundred, thousand, million and so forth), it should be spelt out:

> The first thousand went free; the next hundred had to pay.
>
> The fire destroyed about five thousand books.
>
> She lived and wrote a thousand years ago.

Words should be preferred to figures where inelegance due to mixed forms would otherwise result:

> He asked for ninety dollars and received nine hundred and ninety.

Avoid successive numerals in a single expression:

> 15 two-inch ball-bearings, five three-room apartments

In expressing inclusive numbers falling within the same hundred, the complete number should be given, and not just the last two figures:

> 13–15, 44–47, 100–122, 104–108, 1933–1939

In particular, dates before the Christian era should be stated in full since the shorter form could be misleading:

> Nebuchadnezzar (1792–1750 BC) (not (1792–50 BC))

Numbers up to 999 are written without a comma, like 589; those from 1,000 upwards take a comma, like 125,397; those with seven or more digits take two or more commas, separating groups of three digits counting from the right, for example:

> 9,999,000,000

However, where digits align in columns, in copy such as tables or accounts, commas must be consistently included or omitted in all numbers above 999.[34]

---

34. See *ibid.*, 8.2. My approach on commas in numerals differs from that of the *MHRA Style Guide*.

Always use numerals for ages:

Charles was 25, his sister a mere 16.

A 22-year-old man found a 70-year-old woman yesterday.

Note the use of hyphens in the second example.

Form plurals of spelled-out numbers following the rules for forming the plurals of other nouns.

sixes, hundreds

Never start a sentence with a numeral; either spell it out or rewrite the sentence to avoid this. For a series of specified quantities, use numbers, even for single-digit figures with the exception of one:

In the fire, they reported that 120 were unhurt, 20 were missing, 5 were seriously injured but only one was killed.

In the main body of the text for a single quantity use per cent (not percent and not the % symbol):

The population rose by 54 per cent
45.24 per cent

When many percentages are being given use the % symbol:

Of the remaining 8,200, 26% were from Cavan, 73% were from Mayo and 1% was from Donegal.

Always use the symbol % in the notes.
Do not use the comma and or 'No.' in an address:

10 Downing Street

When making a comparison between quantities one often needs to make a choice between the words fewer and less. Generally, when we're talking about countable things, we use the word fewer; when we're talking about measurable quantities that we cannot count, we use the word less. Use *fewer* when referring to a countable amount that could be expressed as a specific number; *fewer* is used to modify a plural noun. Use *less* when making comparisons that do not lend themselves to numeric amounts. Use less to describe uncountable quantities, collective amounts, and degree; *less* is also used to modify a singular noun. The terms *fewer* and *less* are not interchangeable.

Examples:

I have fewer papers to mark than last year.

She had fewer chores, but she also had less energy.

You'll need less paper if you type your report.

The town spent less than four percent of its budget on snow removal.

Another practical rule to consider is that if you can substitute *much* as the modifier, then use *less;* if you can substitute *many,* use *fewer.*

c) Fractions

Fractions written as words should be hyphenated:

two-thirds, three-fifths

In mathematical material, fractions are written numerically:

¼, ½, ⅔, ¾, ⅘

Decimal points should be marked on the baseline. A zero must precede the decimal point in numbers smaller than 1; but omit zeros after the decimal point unless necessary to indicate exact measurement.

0.67, 0.3, 1.5 (not 1.50)

d) Roman numerals

The use of Roman numerals is usually confined to a few specific purposes:[35]

1. large capitals for the ordinals of monarchs and popes (Edward VII, Pius XII), and for major subdivisions within a text;
2. large capitals for volume numbers of books (journals and series take arabic numerals), also for the acts of plays, for 'books' or other major subdivisions of long poems, novels, and the like, and for certain other documents
3. small capitals for centuries in some languages other than English (XVIe siècle, siglo XVII); however, in Cyrillic script large capitals are used;
4. lower case for the preliminary pages of a book or journal, where these are numbered separately, and for minor subdivisions within a text; inclusive numbers are written out in full, like 'xxiv–xxviii' and not 'xxiv–viii'.

e) Currency

Words should be used to express simple sums of money occurring in normal prose:[36]

> The manuscript was sold for ten shillings in 1965.
> The painting costs twenty-five dollars.
> The fee was three hundred euro.

Names of foreign currencies should be given in their English form where one is in common use, e.g. 'mark' or 'deutschmark' (not 'deutsche Mark'), '[Swedish] crown', and so forth. Note too the use of English plurals such as 'drachmas, pfennigs' (but '[Italian] lire'). Sums of money which are awkward to express in words, or sums occurring in statistical tables, may be written in figures.

35. See *ibid.*, 8.3, with small differences.

36. See *ibid.*, 8.4.

British currency before 1971 should be shown in the following form:

The ring was sold for £197 12s. 6d. in 1965.

British decimal currency should be expressed in pounds and pence separated by a full-stop on the line, not by a comma:

£12.65 (not £12,65 or £12.65p)

Sums below one pound should be shown thus (without a full-stop after 'p'):[37]

84p, 6p

The same conventions apply to sums expressed in euro, dollars, or yen:[38]

€25.46, $500, $8.95, 25c, ¥2000

Where it is necessary to specify that reference is to the American, Canadian, or some other dollar, an appropriate abbreviation precedes the symbol without a full-stop or a space:[39]

US$, CAD$, A$ (or Aus$), NZ$

In most cases, abbreviations for (Swiss) francs, Scandinavian crowns, or pre-2002 European currencies follow the figure, from which they are separated by a space, and are not followed by a full-stop:[40]

95 F, 250 Kr

BF, FF, SwF, DKr, NKr, SKr where it is necessary to specify Belgian, French, Swiss, Danish, Norwegian, or Swedish currency.

---

37. See *ibid.*.
38. See *ibid.*.
39. See *ibid.*.
40. See *ibid.*.

However, the abbreviation 'DM' for the German mark precedes the figure and is separated from it by a space:

DM 8

The names of other currencies are best written out in full:

350 escudos, 500 pesetas, 20 roubles

f) Weights and measures

In non-mathematical contexts one should express weights and measures in words:[41]

The recipe for *Absinthe Martini* takes only two ounces of gin.

In statistical works or in subjects where frequent reference is made to them, weights and measures may be expressed in figures with appropriate abbreviations:[42]

The priory is situated 3 km from the village of Crowthorne.

The same 12 mm capitals were used by three Berlin printers at different times.

Where measurements of temperature are abbreviated, the symbol belongs with the abbreviation, and the abbreviation takes no point.

10°C, 87°F

Note that most of these abbreviations do not take a full-stop or plural 's': 1 kg, 15 kg, 1 mm, 6 cm, 15 m, 4 l (litres), 2 ft, 100 lb, 10 oz, but, to avoid ambiguity, use 'in.' for 'inch(es)'.

---

41. See *ibid.*, 8.5.

42. See *ibid.*.

2.3 Stylistic hints

2.3.1 Basic points

While a great work of literature is rarely encountered in a thesis, certain *stylistic* hints should be borne in mind.

Repetition of words or phrases should be avoided within a given paragraph. A thesaurus should be employed if necessary; many word-processing programs are equipped with one. Conciseness is intimately connected to clarity, and remains a struggle for every writer. Given that writing is a gradual and spontaneous activity, assignments come into being with a great deal of stress and mess. As our ideas swirl around us, and as we struggle to give them order, clarity, and vigour, our words swirl around us, too. It is typical for good writers to produce wordy early drafts, and then work through several stages of revision to find and eliminate all the excess. Richard Lanham says that writing typically starts out with a high 'lard factor', as he calls it—the number of words in one's first draft minus the number of words in one's revision, divided by the number of words in the original. As a rule of thumb, Lanham says, 'think of a lard factor of one-third to one-half as normal and don't stop revising until you've removed it'.[43]

Many students are so accustomed to padding their writing that it's hard even to imagine how to cut the surplus. Writing to required page lengths is one of the reasons many writers are good at wordiness. Sometimes, though, wordiness just seems to happen. It can start with doubling of words. Instead of 'mutual agreement', simply use 'agreement'. Instead of 'future prospects' just 'prospects'. 'Whether or not' can be reduced to 'whether'. Error is generally inadvertent, so the expression 'inadvertent error' can simply become 'error'.

43. R. A. Lanham, *Revising Prose* (New York: Macmillan, 1992), p. 4.

Here's a typical example from a corporate technical manual. The passage specifies the protocol for tracking changes in an accounting system:

> To ensure that the new system being developed, or the existing system being modified, will provide users with the timely, accurate, and complete information they require to properly perform their functions and responsibilities, it is necessary to assure that the new or modified system will cover all necessary aspects of the present automated or manual systems being replaced. To gain this assurance, it is essential that documentation be made of the entities of the present systems which will be modified or eliminated.

Revising this isn't easy. For one thing, what information can be dispensed with, and what should be preserved? Is it important, for instance, to note that information should be 'timely, accurate, and complete'? Or is this obvious from the context? There's no absolute right answer. It depends on what your own ideas are, and what your readers expect. Here's one possible revision that maintains a fairly formal tone:

> To ensure that users have all the information needed to do their jobs, the new system must preserve the present system's critical functions. Therefore, all modifications to the present system must be documented.

Here is a slightly less formal version:

> Make sure to document all changes to the current system, so that all original functions can be recovered if necessary.

Here is another example:

> The last point I would like to make is that in regard to men-women relationships, it is important to keep in mind that the greatest changes have probably occurred in the way men and women are working next to one another.

The sentence can be revised as follows:

> The greatest changes in how men and women treat each other have probably occurred in the workplace.

Avoid beginning sentences with 'And', 'But' or with a numeral. Instead of 'And' use 'Moreover' or 'Furthermore'. In place of 'But' employ 'However'. Never use 'etcetera' or etc. at the end of sentence; this indicates a lack of knowledge. A reference would probably help at this point, or else a formulation with the word 'including'. Another abbreviation to be avoided is 'e.g.', which should simply be substituted with 'for example' or 'such as'. Instead of 'viz', adopt 'namely' or 'for instance'. The abbreviation 'i.e.' should be replaced by 'that is' or 'therefore'. The expression 'in fact' should simply be omitted wherever possible. On the other hand, the terms 'indeed', 'thus' and 'therefore' may be used, albeit sparingly.

The use of language should be optimised in order to convey the desired meaning in the minimum number of words. Know how to use the right images, in order to say what you mean and mean what you say. A check should be made to see if the expression is clear. It is wise to come back to the written work after a suitable period of time has elapsed, in order to gain distance from it. Alternatively, the comments of a friend or colleague may be helpful.

Care should be taken to ensure that quotations really fit in with the flow of the text. Quotations are a minefield. There are a thousand things that can go wrong—putting too much stress on quotations, quoting too much, quoting the wrong passages, blurring the line between your voice and those of the sources you quote, disrupting the flow of your argument, and so on. Quoting too much is one of the commonest mistakes inexperienced writers make, as if they think it's disrespectful to an original text to cut it into small pieces. However, there's nothing disrespectful about helping a quote make an emphatic point. Whenever you quote, be aware of what you're looking for, and try to seize upon a sharp and pithy excerpt.

The text should be even and consistent in its style; there should be no foreign bodies of irrelevant material or embroidery in the writing. A thesis is not the same literary genre as a novel! Vigorous writing is concise. A sentence should contain no unnecessary words, a paragraph no unnecessary sentences, for the same reason that a drawing should have no unnecessary lines and a machine no unnecessary parts. This requires not that the writer make all his sentences short, or that he avoid all detail and treat his subjects only in outline, but that every word be full of meaning.

Many expressions in common use violate this principle. In particular, the expression 'the fact that' should be revised out of every sentence in which it occurs.

Phrase	Revision
the question as to whether	Whether (the question whether)
used for fuel purposes	used for fuel
he is a man who	he
in a hasty manner	hastily
this is a subject which	this subject
there is no doubt but that	doubtless
His story is a strange one.	His story is strange.

The excessive use of relative structures renders sentences weak or bloated. Expressions like who is, which was, are often superfluous.

Instead of:

His brother, who is a member of the same firm.

Revise to:

His brother, a member of the same firm.

Instead of:

Trafalgar, which was Nelson's last battle.

Revise to:

Trafalgar, Nelson's last battle

Instead of:

The novel, which is entitled Ulysses, takes place.

Revise to:

The novel Ulysses takes place.

Instead of:

It was Nelson who said

Revise to:

Nelson said

Instead of:

I think that X is the case

Revise to:

X is the case, as this evidence shows:

Instead of:

There is a tendency among many writers who may be seen to display certain signs of lack of confidence that their sentences will be overloaded with relative clauses and other words which are generally useless in function.

Revise to:

Many hesitant writers overload their sentences with relative clauses and other useless words.

A further problem is the employment of passive verbs, which should be changed to the active voice, if possible with a personal subject.

Weak:

It is felt that an exercise program should be attempted by this patient before any surgery is performed.

Improved:

The patient should attempt an exercise program before surgery.

Weak:

The bevelling jig is said by most users to be faulty.

Improved:

Most users say the bevelling jig is faulty.

A common violation of conciseness is the presentation of a single complex idea, step by step, in a series of sentences which might to advantage be combined into one.

Long sentence:

Macbeth was very ambitious. This led him to wish to become king of Scotland. The witches told him that this wish of his would come true. The king of Scotland at this time was Duncan. Encouraged by his wife, Macbeth murdered Duncan. He was thus enabled to succeed Duncan as king. (55 words.)

Revision:

> Encouraged by his wife, Macbeth achieved his ambition and realized the prediction of the witches by murdering Duncan and becoming king of Scotland in his place. (26 words.)

The ability to write a good parallel sentence is invaluable in essay work. Parallelism is one of the most useful and flexible techniques. It refers to any structure which brings together parallel elements, be these nouns, adjectives, verbs, adverbs, or larger structures. Done well, parallelism imparts grace and power to passages:

> The prince's strength is also his weakness; his self-reliance is also isolation.

Faulty parallelism, on the other hand, produces an effect in your reader similar to changing gears without using the clutch. A successful parallel sentence reads smoothly, while a faulty parallel sentence lurches awkwardly. The previous sentence is an example of good parallelism because it obeys the technique's central rule: The grammatical elements of parallel clauses must match. The following sentence is an example of poor parallelism because the verb form changes:

> This is a debate begun in Greece and which continues into modern times.

'Begun' is a participial adjective while 'continues' is an active verb. The sentence should read:

> This debate began in Greece and continues into modern times.

The rule applies not only to verbs but also to nouns, adjectives, adverbs and other parts of speech. In the following sentence, for example, a noun has been mixed with a pair of verbal nouns (gerunds):

> I acquired my considerable fortune by investing carefully, hard work and marrying a rich woman.

The sentence should read:

> I acquired my considerable fortune by investing carefully, working hard and marrying a rich woman.

Clichés should be avoided. Most clichés were once pithy, clever sayings in which someone encapsulated an idea or feeling. Unfortunately, thousands of other people used and reused those sayings, until they became hackneyed, trite and tiresome. Because they are catchy and concise, clichés stick in the brain and immediately occur to the stymied writer. However, using a worn-out phrase is tantamount to admitting that you have not been able to think of anything more interesting to say. Don't be deceived into thinking that if you put quotation marks around a cliché it suddenly becomes respectable. On the contrary, you will simply convince your reader that you ran out of ideas. Some clichés to avoid include the following:

> avoid like the plague, better late than never,
> bright and early, butterflies in my stomach,
> cool as a cucumber, death warmed up,
> easier said than done, far and few between,
> green with envy, hotter than hell, in this day and age,
> last but not least, laughing like a hyena, lazy as sin,
> like water off a duck's back, long-lost, love at first sight,
> proud as a peacock, selling like hotcakes,
> sleep like a log, slowly but surely, sweating like a pig,
> white as a sheet, work like a dog.

Stock phrases like these are also best used as little as possible:

> within the framework of, at this point in time,
> in the final analysis, at the earliest possible moment,

as a matter of fact, relieved of the position,
a steep learning curve.

Jargon is unnecessarily technical language which provides polysyllabic replacements for perfectly adequate simple words. Organizations such as the military and the government are renowned for their ability to bury simple statements under a ton of verbiage. The process seems to arise from a fear that official proclamations do not sound official enough. Jargon is also used to make something unpalatable sound more acceptable. In the 1991 Gulf War, the phrase 'collateral damage' was coined by the military to avoid having to admit that even the smartest bomb caused civilian causalities; similarly, while the transformation of 'dustman' into 'sanitation engineer' or 'ecological worker' removes the sexist connotation of the original, it is also an attempt to cover up the verbal smell of refuse. In both these examples, the initial urge to create the jargon came from the desire to make something unpleasant seem acceptable; many euphemisms of this kind give an impression of insincerity at the same time as generating wordiness: 'passed away' for 'died', 'comfort station' for 'lavatory', and so on.

Increasing specialization in our society contributes to the spread of jargon, a substantial portion of which is derived from technical vocabulary. Many of these new words are necessary in their original contexts, but they have also begun to creep into areas where they are unappreciated. Computer terms such as 'interface' and 'output' can be confusing when applied to real life. Literary criticism is a rich source of jargon, and businesses are particularly guilty of creating terms that are meaningless in their generality (like 'functional management options').

The one grammatical characteristic of jargon that is readily identifiable is the suffix 'ise'. Words such as 'systematized' and 'prioritised' permeate official writing, resulting in the creation of such unnecessary synonyms as 'finalize' (for 'finish') and the popular 'utilize', which appears to be trying to erase 'use' from the face of the earth. Avoid the frequent use (not 'utilization') of 'ise' words; they are pretentious, and there are probably simpler words that accomplish the same task. Jargon is intended to impress, but it also seems intended to intimidate and confuse. It can also be unintentionally comic, if it is used in a context where it is clearly inappropriate.

Even the most pithy historical phrases can be rendered innocuous by jargon phraseology. For example, Julius Caesar's boasts 'I came, I saw, I conquered' ('*Veni, vidi, vici*') when rendered into socspeak become:

> Upon the advent of the investigator, his hegemony became minimally coextensive with the areal unit rendered visible by his successive displacements in space.[44]

A further current trap for writers is politically-correct language. Politically-correct restrictions on what we can say and how we say it have been imposed by custom and convention.

> Political correctness is the communal tyranny that erupted in the 1980s. It was a spontaneous declaration that particular ideas, expressions and behaviour, which were then legal, should be forbidden by law, and people who transgressed should be punished. It started with a few voices but grew in popularity until it became unwritten and written law within the community. With those who were publicly declared as being not politically correct becoming the object of persecution by the mob, if not prosecution by the state.[45]

---

44. See M. Cowley, 'Sociological Habit Patterns In Linguistic Transmogrification' in *The Reporter* (20 September 1956), p. 43.
45. P. Atkinson, 'The origin and nature of political correctness.' *Civilization defined and explained in plain English*. Web. 21

Political correctness can be traced back to Germany of the 1920s, where Communist academics sought to impose their Marxist views on students. The modern politically correct movement began at the University of Wisconsin-Madison. To get an idea of how ridiculous this can become, consider the following politically correct rendering of the fairy-tale *Little Red Riding Hood*:

> **Female gender in red hemp cloth hood**
>
> There once was a young person named Little Red Riding Hood who lived on the edge of a large forest full of endangered owls and rare plants that would probably provide a cure for cancer if only someone took the time to study them. Red Riding Hood lived with a nurture giver whom she sometimes referred to as 'mother', although she didn't mean to imply by this term that she would have thought less of the person if a close biological link did not in fact exist. Nor did she intend to denigrate the equal value of nontraditional households, although she was sorry if this was the impression conveyed. One day her mother asked her to take a basket of organically grown fruit and mineral water to the house of her grandmother (or more accurately nurturing matriarch). She said, 'But mother, won't this be stealing work from the unionised people who have struggled for years to earn the right to carry all packages between various people in the woods?' Red Riding Hood's mother assured her that she had called the union chief and obtained a special compassionate mission exemption form. 'But mother, aren't you oppressing me by ordering me to do this?'
>
> Red Riding Hood's mother pointed out that it was impossible for women to oppress each other, since all women were equally oppressed until all women were free 'But mother, then shouldn't you have my brother carry the basket, since he's an oppressor, and should learn what it's like to be oppressed?' And Red Riding Hood's mother

---

December 2009. <http://ourcivilisation.com/pc.htm>.

> explained that her brother was attending a special rally for animal rights, and besides, this wasn't stereotypical women's work, but an empowering deed that would help engender a feeling of community. 'But won't I be oppressing Grandma, by implying that she's sick and hence unable to independently further her own selfhood?' Red Riding Hood's mother explained that her grandmother wasn't actually sick or incapacitated or mentally handicapped in any way, although that was not to imply that any of these conditions were inferior to what some people called 'health'.[46]

2.3.2 *Grammar and Usage*

Even the most seasoned writers routinely make mistakes. Below are some common grammatical errors that should be avoided.

a) Dangling Modifiers

A modifier is a word or phrase that qualifies the meaning of another word, phrase, or clause. A dangling modifier is a qualifier that has been misplaced.

> Incorrect: On arriving at the station, the bulletin board informed us the train was late.

Because the bulletin board did not arrive at the station, the modifier is in the wrong place.

> Correct: On arriving at the station, we learned from the bulletin board that the train was late.

Here is another example:

> Incorrect: In cooperation with hospital, state, and industrial organizations, studies are being made of problems in occupational health, nutrition, and heart disease.

---

46. Adapted from J. F. Garner, *Politically Correct Bedtime Stories* (Hoboken, NJ: John Wiley & Sons, 1994).

Correct: In cooperation with hospital, state, and industrial organizations, the institute is studying problems in occupational health, nutrition, and heart disease.

b) Misplaced Modifiers

In the following sentence, the modifying phrase has been misplaced:

> Growing at the bottom of the glass, Alison found some mould.

Since it is the mould that is growing at the bottom of the glass, rather than Alison, the sentence should read:

> Alison found some mould growing at the bottom of the glass.

c) Squinting Modifier

A squinting modifier appears in the middle of the sentence, where its object is not clear: 'I said eventually I would do it.' The writer could mean:

> 'Eventually, I said I would do it.'

or

> 'I said I would do it eventually.'

d) Sentence fragments

Fragments are incomplete sentences. Usually, fragments are pieces of sentences that have become disconnected from the main clause. One of the easiest ways to correct them is to remove the full-stop between the fragment and the main clause. Other kinds of punctuation may be needed for the newly combined sentence. One case is where there is no subject-verb relationship:

Example:

> Working far into the night in an effort to salvage her little boat.

This could be re-written as follows:

> She worked far into the night in an effort to salvage her little boat.

Another case may even have a subject-verb relationship, but it has been subordinated to another idea by a dependent word and so cannot stand by itself:

Example:

> Even though he had the better arguments and was by far the more powerful speaker.

This sentence fragment has a subject 'he', and two verbs, 'had' and 'was', but it cannot stand by itself because of the dependent word (subordinating conjunction) 'even though'. An independent clause is needed to follow up this dependent clause:

> Even though he had the better arguments and was by far the more powerful speaker, he lost the case because he didn't understand the jury.

e) Faulty Reference of Pronouns

When a pronoun (like 'them') doesn't agree with the noun to which it refers (like 'the official'), this is noun-pronoun disagreement.

> Incorrect: Every full-time undergraduate is eligible for office and every one of them votes.

In this case, 'them' does not match the noun it refers to, 'undergraduate'.

> Correct: Every full-time undergraduate is eligible for office, and every one votes.

f) Disagreement of Subject and Verb

The number of the verb depends on the number of the subject.

> Incorrect: These notes should be read carefully before the directories or roster are used.

The verb should agree with the nearer of two subjects joined by 'or'.

> Correct: These notes should be read carefully before the directories and roster are used.

Phrases introduced by 'as well as' or any of the following expressions do not affect the number of the subject when they separate it from the verb: accompanied by, along with, besides, followed by, in addition to, including, no less than, plus, rather than, together with, with.

g) Lack of Parallel Structure

Parallel constructions require that expressions similar in content and function be outwardly similar. That is, similar groups of ideas should be treated the same way.

> Incorrect: The school accepts not only transfer students but encourages part-time students as well.

The parts after 'not only' and 'but also' must match-but they don't.

> Correct: The school not only accepts transfer students but also encourages part-time students.

Here is another example of a lack of parallel structure:

> Incorrect: Not only are we paying for our daughter's wedding but also for the honeymoon.

There should be either two prepositional phrases or two independent clauses after the two parts of the correlative conjunction, but not one clause and one phrase.

Correct: We are paying not only for our daughter's wedding but also for the honeymoon.

Also correct: Not only are we paying for our daughter's wedding, but we are also paying for the honeymoon.

h) Illogical Grouping

Similar to a lack of parallelism, an illogical grouping is a series of words that doesn't make sense.

Incorrect: Generals Lois, Clarke, and Admiral Halsey

Because Admiral Halsey is not a general like Lois and Clarke, the grouping must be rewritten.

Correct: Generals Lois and Clarke and Admiral Halsey.

i) Balancing a sentence

It is important to ensure that a sentence balances on either side of certain words (correlatives) that emphasize similarity or contrast and that are used in parallel: both and and; either and or; neither and nor; not only and but; between and and; whether and or. For example:

'I swam both in the morning and afternoon'

should read

'I swam both in the morning and in the afternoon'

or

'I swam in both the morning and the afternoon'.

Note the position of the preposition 'in'.

j) Split Infinitives

Split infinitives occur when additional words are included between to and the verb in an infinitive. Many readers find a single adverb splitting the infinitive to be acceptable, but this practice should be avoided in formal writing, unless the alternative seems excessively awkward or clumsy.

Example:

Acceptable in informal contexts:

> I needed to quickly gather my personal possessions.

Revised for formal contexts:

> I needed to gather my personal possessions quickly.

There are occasions when splitting the infinitive is far clearer than any alternative phrasing:

Examples:

> That was the only way to more than double his salary.

> We expect our output to more than triple in a year

k) 'That' versus 'Which'

Substitute 'that' for 'which' in restrictive clauses. Here is a useful rule of thumb: 'that' should be used for defining clauses and 'which' for non-defining clauses. If 'which' is appropriate, it is always preceded by a comma.

> The poker group that meets on Tuesday evening makes a very fine nacho dip.

This is a defining clause—that is, out of all the poker groups, the one that meets Tuesday evening concocts the best chip dip.

> The poker group, which meets on Tuesday evening, makes a very fine nacho dip.

In this case, there is only one poker group, and, incidentally, it meets Tuesday evening.

l) Redundancy

Avoid using a modifying word when the intended meaning is inherent in a word already used. Redundancy is obvious in examples such as:

> the results were plotted graphically
> past history
> bright blue in colour
> inactivates its activity
> completely filled

Does the term 'careful monitoring' suggest that the alternative is careless monitoring?

m) Non sequiturs

Look out for text that does not logically follow what goes before as in the following example:

> Forage turnip is widely grown in northern Europe, but it is distributed over much of northern Asia, northern North America and southern Oceania.

This should have read:

> Forage turnip is widely grown in northern Europe **and** is also distributed over much of northern Asia, northern North America and southern Oceania.

n) The historical present

One convention in academic writing that often gives students difficulty is which tense to use when discussing a text. One's first inclination is probably to use the past tense when discussing a book written in the past. However, that's not what is always done. Most textual analysis and commentary is written in the present tense, a convention sometimes called the historical present:

Original:

> Hamlet told Ophelia he never loved her.

Revision:

Hamlet tells Ophelia he never loved her.

Nevertheless, to complicate matters, you don't always use the present tense in discussing a work. When you're presenting facts on its composition, you should use the past tense:

Original:

Machiavelli writes *The Prince* in 1513.

Revision:

Machiavelli wrote *The Prince* in 1513.

3 THE ESSAY

I am convinced more and more day by day that fine writing is next to fine doing.

John Keats, *Letter to J. H. Reynolds*

If any man wish to write in a clear style, let him be first clear in his thoughts; and if any would write in a noble style, let him first possess a noble soul.

Johann Wolfgang von Goethe

3.1 Basic ideas

The word essay derives from the French infinitive *essayer*, 'to try' or 'to attempt'. The expression, in turn, stems from the late Latin expression *exagiare* which means 'to weigh', close to the idea of weighing something up. The French form of the word also comes from the Latin verb *exigere*, which means 'to examine, test, or to inquire about'.[1] Through the excavation of this ancient term, we are able to unearth the essence of the academic essay: to encourage students to test or examine their ideas concerning a particular topic. Student essays are usually designed to foster exploration of a new topic or to test understanding of course material. The student will be expected to weigh up different views, theories or pieces of evidence. The following reflections are intended to help the writer of an essay to make the attempt a good one. Many rules for writing an essay also apply to a seminar paper, a term paper, an *elaboratum* or an article

1. See *Oxford Latin Dictionary* (Oxford: University Press, 1968), p. 643.

for a journal. A seminar provides training in two basic scientific skills. One is how to present a scientific paper at a conference or congress, the second is how to prepare a paper for publication in a learned journal, or in the acts or proceedings of a congress. The same fundamental methodological skills employed here will later be applied to writing a thesis or even an academic textbook.

An essay or seminar paper, often 10–15 pages long with double-spacing, is a work of synthesis which constitutes a proof of the ability to introduce a theme and develop it to its logical conclusions. Thus, it is helpful to make an outline plan before beginning to write the text. It is also an exercise of the ability to prepare a bibliography and notes, bearing in mind the golden rules of consistency and coherence, which have been described above. If English is not your first language, be sure that you have someone to correct your text before you present it. In this way, you will be sure that you are really writing what you really mean.

The essay lies at the heart of some of the most useful skills gained through education. The subject is only broadly defined. It can be anything, from contemporary Slavonic literature, to the rise and fall of an ancient empire, to a theological overview of original sin. Your first task is to ferret out a subject or topic, and hopefully an interesting one, from all the information available. You study this topic, pursuing false leads and true, until you have enough to write about in a reasoned and orderly manner. In short, you learn how to research, and then how to articulate what you have learned. The world abounds in ambiguity, the same ambiguity that you face at the outset of a research project. Many people are intimidated by what they don't know, are apprehensive of delving into things beyond their experience. The research experience teaches you there is order lurking somewhere out there in the unknown, and that you can find it, or better still, elaborate it. This is not a small thing to learn. Do not underestimate the value of your time and interest. A good teacher will assign you a manageable subject, neither so broad as to overwhelm you, nor so narrow as to limit your freedom of expression. Moreover they will guide you through the research process.

3.1.1 Getting started

Writing an essay is hard work. However, experience suggests there are two tasks that cause undue frustration. The first is choosing a topic. The second is making the transition from research to writing. Intelligent students have long known how to solve these problems. If you have never written a paper, perhaps you cannot appreciate these challenges. Your first task is to take the assignment as given by your instructor and develop for yourself an appropriate topic. How do you to figure out what is an appropriate topic without first doing some research? Then again, how can you to do some useful research without first defining the appropriate topic? This is a classic double-bind, a vicious circle, a true *Catch-22* situation.[2] As a consequence many students agonize over choosing a topic—with insufficient knowledge to do so effectively—paralysed from getting on with the project at the very first step. Like a rabbit caught in the headlights of a car, they freeze as they run out of time. It is not that they are lazy, they just don't know how and where to get started.

---

2. A Catch-22 situation, coined by Joseph Heller in his novel *Catch-22*, is a logical paradox where an individual finds him or herself in need of something that can be had only by not being in need of it. It is often cited with regard to rules, regulations, procedures, or situations in which one has knowledge of being or becoming a victim, but has no control over it occurring.

The secret to getting started is to find one good source. There are places to look right in your library that can get your project off to a good start. This old approach may be the quickest way to get your paper off the ground. Once started with the research, when do you stop though? Once you have collected all of your information, you must begin to think about organizing it and putting it in written form. How do you know when you have collected all the information you will need? How much research is enough? When do you stop researching and start writing? How do you start writing? Does this sound familiar? You've done a great job with your research. You have dutifully photocopied and highlighted twenty fine sources. Now you are ready to write, but nothing happens. You stare at the screen of your word processor, then at your stack of photocopies. You write a couple of sentences or paragraphs, then start sifting through your sources for something you recall as important. You find it, but can't remember why it was important, and so start rereading the paper. And so it continues.

Perhaps only one or two paragraphs make it to the screen after an hour's work. You need to get this paper done, but you are going nowhere, fast. And, it doesn't seem to be getting any easier. You need to get organized. The secret of getting organized is to develop an annotated bibliography. An annotated bibliography is composed of your own notes—all that you found important when you first read and evaluated a source. By taking good notes you begin writing your paper when you start reading your first research source. Your notes can be organized to produce the outline for your paper. This is why we emphasized the use of note cards back in chapter one.

3.1.2 First impressions

They say that first impressions are quite important when meeting a new person. It takes just a quick glance, maybe three seconds, for someone to evaluate you when you meet for the first time. In this short time, the other person forms an opinion about you based on your appearance, your body language, your demeanour, your mannerisms, and how you are dressed. The professor or examiner evaluating the essay, as well as the casual reader will be looking for these key 'first impressions' in an essay. First of all, clear English is a must, and what was outlined in the previous chapter should be taken into account. After that, the reader should be able to pick up the writer's capacity to answer the question at hand. Each stage of the argument should be supported by evidence. The writer shows great acumen if he or she has read round the subject, and thought laterally, rather than just repeating information mechanically from one lecture or one course book.[3] A fine essay should be occasions for its author to manifest signs of reflection, to think about the evidence and theories under consideration and treat them objectively and critically. An essay needs to treat the underlying issues and ideas that relate to the question, without getting lost in excessive detail, so as to demonstrate understanding of those issues and ideas. The references in an essay furnish evidence that the writer knows who also treated these issues and ideas and when, where, why and how. An essay needs to deal with an accurate analysis of the theme and not just description, in a precise and not a generalized way.

---

3. Lateral thinking is a term coined by Edward de Bono in the book *New Think: The Use of Lateral Thinking* published in 1967; it refers to solving problems through an indirect and creative approach. Lateral thinking is about reasoning that is not immediately obvious and about ideas that may not be obtainable by using only traditional step-by-step logic.

A well-groomed essay manifests signs of editing, namely seeing if the material is in the best possible order. You need to ask whether the words are really saying what you want to say. Revising gives you the chance to preview your work on behalf of the eventual reader. Revision is much more than proofreading, though in the final editing stage it involves some checking of details. Good revision and editing can transform a mediocre first draft into an excellent final paper. It's more work, but leads to real satisfaction when you find you've said what you wanted. Revision may mean changing the form and reasoning in your essay. It often means adding or deleting sentences and paragraphs, shifting them around, and reshaping them as you go. Before dealing with details of style and language (editing), be sure you have presented ideas that are clear and forceful. Make notes as you go through these questions, and stop after each section to make the desired revisions.

Of course, before handing in a piece of written work (and this doesn't just apply to the student scene), it should be proof read, so as to avoid presenting something that's full of grammar, punctuation and spelling mistakes. The person reading and marking it will just assume you couldn't be bothered with your essay. Here, it's also clear that spelling and grammar checking tools in word-processing packages will not do the job for you.

3.1.3 Personal or impersonal?

One of the most frequently asked questions by essay writers is 'should I use the personal pronoun in my writing?' The answer is that there is no single easy answer. Some subjects encourage the use of 'I' while others actually frown on it or 'ban' its use because it is thought to show a lack of objectivity. Some lecturers don't mind but others will mark students down. So, one way to answer this question is first, to find out what the convention is in your subject; and then ask your teachers what they expect to see in the essays they set you.

Clearly, an essay is not the same as a newspaper or popular magazine article, although the boundaries between the two literary genres are becoming increasingly blurred. Part of the reason for this is the amount of information published on the Internet in the form of blogs; the blog tends to transcend established forms of writing.[4]

Sometimes it can be appropriate to use personal experience or to use a personal tone in an essay. Imagine you were studying for joint honours in theology and Christian art and that you had spent a semester working in Rome. In your final year, you decide to write a long essay about how an aspect of Christian art reflects theology. Here the personal could well be appropriate. In your introduction, you might announce that the essay is going to use the theories of various theologians and art historians; however you could also say that you are going to test some of these ideas against your own Roman experiences. However, you have to judge whether it's appropriate to do so or not—and, of course, find out whether your professor or tutor will welcome such an approach.

One reason for not using 'I', and one reason why many teachers seem to dislike it, is that it shows a lack of objectivity. Consider the analogy of the detective: he does not say 'I think John Smith is guilty' but rather 'The evidence points to the fact that John Smith is guilty'.

4. A blog, a contraction of the term 'web log', is part of a web site. Blogs are usually maintained by an individual with regular entries of commentary, descriptions of events, or other material such as graphics or video. Many blogs provide commentary or news on a particular theme; others function as more personal online diaries. The ability of readers to leave comments in an interactive format is an important part of many blogs.

Another reason for not using 'I' is that once you start, it is very easy to slip into a chatty and even intimate style like that of a 'blog'; and once you've slipped into a chatty style, it's even easier to start offering opinions at the level of feelings and prejudices. A typical example would be 'Professor Smith's theory says this but what I think…'. Examiners who mark essays are less interested in what a student thinks than in what he knows, or in what he has found out. To put that another way, they are more interested in one's ability to exercise judgement than to proffer opinions.

An impersonal style uses the passive voice, the third person rather than the first person (it rather than I or we), and employs things rather than people as subjects of sentences. However, overuse of the passive voice may mean that your writing is less precise, and it may lead to writing which is more difficult to read because it is less natural than the active voice. Times are changing, and in some disciplines it is now quite acceptable to use the active voice, personal pronouns such as 'I' and 'we', and to use people as subjects of sentences.

The basic question is: Does a personal tone add anything useful to the essay? Here we can take a point from an imaginary essay and look at the two styles of writing it.

Examples:

Impersonal tone:

> Indeed, some of the more interesting criticism of Balthasar is no longer coming out of the *Concilium* wing of American Catholicism, but from the Thomistic or traditionalist wing. Thomas Weinandy, for instance, in numerous articles and books has mounted a sustained and intelligent defence of the classical understanding of divine immutability, and

with it, a defence of the notion that on the cross it is only the humanity of Christ that suffers.

Personal tone:

> First, one of the reasons that I began this study the way I did was to show just how wedded in many ways Balthasar's thought is to that of Thomas Aquinas. I repeat, for instance, that the entire first volume of *Theo-Logic* reads like an extended commentary on Aquinas's, *On Truth*. Furthermore, in spite of the fact that Thomas does not make Balthasar's famous list of clerical styles that makes up the second volume of *The Glory of the Lord,* he is more than compensated by playing the pivotal role in the two volumes on metaphysics which come later.

These two styles are adopted in the same work, and the more personal style is used towards the later part, by way of a conclusion.

3.1.4 Brainstorming

There is some advantage in writing the basic skeleton of the essay in one sitting, because this can provide it with a unitary feel. This does not mean staying up all night to do it. One method which may help is brainstorming, which signifies attempting to find a solution to a problem or question by collecting spontaneous ideas. Brainstorming is very useful in overcoming that 'rabbit in the headlights' feeling we all get when first faced with an essay title. Brainstorming will help you get past the sensation that you can't start writing until you know what the first sentence is going to be. Brainstorming helps you realise you can 'just start writing'. It is of course true that some tutors don't favour this technique. They complain that it encourages disorganised thinking and therefore disorganised writing so that some student essays look as if they are all storm and no brain.

However, brainstorming can be adjusted to be the more organized first stage of an essay writing process. In this case, brainstorming means taking a pen and paper and writing quickly and intensively for a short period of time. There is no need to worry about getting things in a particular order: it's important just get as much down on paper as one can. Some students prefer to write continuously, to just start and keep going in one great big sentence. Some people prefer to make very quick lists of points under headings. Other people prefer to organise their ideas visually. They might take a big sheet of paper and divide it into three horizontal areas, one for each of the key areas in the essay. They would then group short notes around those topics. It's best to experiment and find the way that works best for you. There are two types of brainstorming, positive and negative.

With positive brainstorming, you take a pen and a sheet of paper and spend a fixed amount of time, like an hour, writing down everything you know and think about a subject. For example, you might start by trying to write quick definitions of all the key terms in the question. Then you might recall material from lectures and seminars dealing with the theme. Finally you would write down all the main texts (books and articles) on the topic that you are able to remember. So this process will help you to access things you already know; and it will help you to think about where to obtain evidence to back up what you know.

In negative brainstorming, you take another sheet of paper and spend another hour writing down everything you don't know about the question, what you still need to find out and what you are going to research. For example, in your positive brainstorm you might have written about some aspects of the theme but you might know nothing about other aspects. On this sheet, you need to jot down where you might find further material. You might start by noting names of likely journals, databases, articles or names of likely books. This is also the place to ask yourself questions about what you don't know. This will help you to think about how to use all the resources that are available.

Brainstorming is a bit like cooking something you've never cooked before. First, you look at the recipe to see what ingredients and equipment are needed. Second, you look in your cupboards and fridge to see what ingredients and equipment you've already got. Third, you make a list of those ingredients and equipment you need to buy.

Some people like to brainstorm visually by writing the key topic in the middle of the page and grouping notes around it. Clusters, mind maps and spider diagrams are more sophisticated ways of doing this. A mind map is a diagram used to represent words, ideas, tasks or other items linked to and arranged radially around a central key word or idea. It is used to generate, visualize, structure and classify ideas, and as an aid to study, organization, problem solving, and decision making. It is an image-centered diagram that represents semantic or other connections between portions of information. By presenting these connections in a radial, non-linear graphical manner, it encourages a brainstorming approach to any given organisational task, eliminating the hurdle of initially establishing an intrinsically appropriate or relevant conceptual framework to work within. A mind map is similar to a semantic network or cognitive map but there are no formal restrictions on the kinds of links used. Most often the map involves images, words, and lines. The elements are arranged intuitively according to the importance of the concepts and they are organized into groupings, branches, or areas. The uniform graphic formulation of the semantic structure of information on the method of gathering knowledge, may aid recall of existing memories.

Mind maps (or similar concepts) have been used for centuries, for learning, brainstorming, memory, visual thinking, and problem-solving by educators, engineers, psychologists and people in general. Some of the earliest examples of mind maps were developed by Porphyry of Tyros, a noted thinker of the third century as he graphically visualised the concept categories of Aristotle. Ramon Llull (1235–1315) also employed these structures of the mind map form.[5] In the late 1950s, semantics studies were developed to investigate human understanding; Allan Collins and M. Ross Qullian evolved mind mapping during the 1960s. The modern claim to the origin of the mind map has been made by a British popular psychology author, Tony Buzan.[6]

Try to place main topic of the essay in the middle of a sheet of paper and draw a circle round it. Then think about ways you could break the main subject down and write these around the circled main term. Draw boxes around these terms and connect them to the main one with lines or arrows. Then repeat the process for this second set of terms. Clusters, mind maps and spider diagrams are particularly helpful for exploring different areas of your subject and thinking about links between them. These techniques can be employed to think about the main events in the plot of a novel, or the main differences and similarities between two management theories. Useful free mind mapping software may be obtained at freemind.sourceforge.net

5. See, for example, R. Llull, *Tree of the Philosophy of Love.*
6. See T. Buzan, *The Mind Map Book* (London: Penguin Books, 1996).

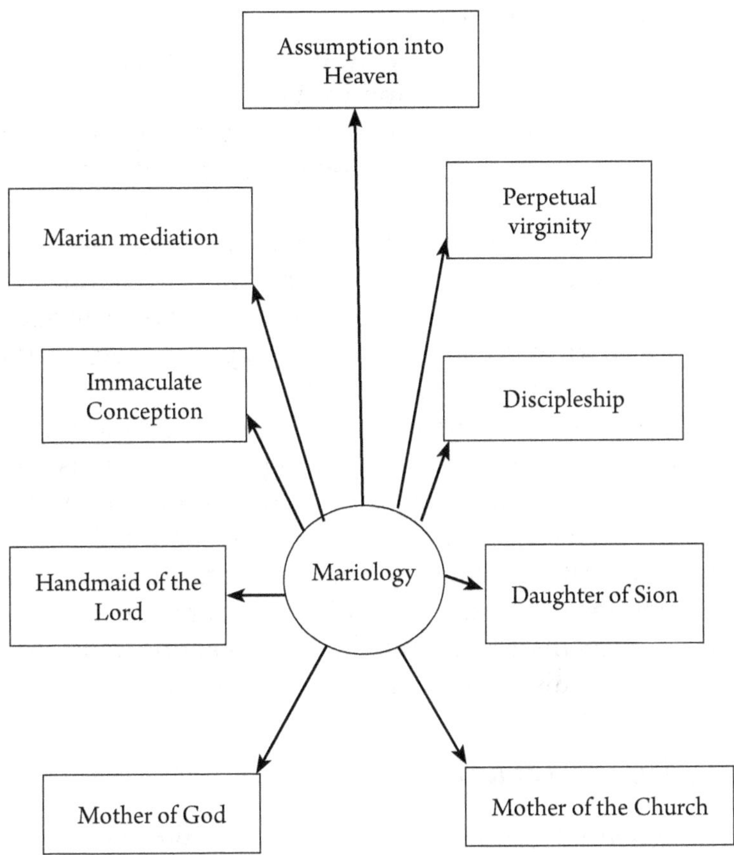

A simple mind map for a Mariology essay

3.1.5 The plan

The foregoing discussion concerning brainstorming leads to the formulation of a plan for the essay. It is very important that you plan your essay, so that you have an idea of what you are going to write before you start to write it. Of course, you will most likely change the material in later drafts, but you should still start off by having a plan in mind. It is very important that your essay has some discernible structure, namely that it is composed of parts and that these parts are logically connected. This helps both you and your reader to be clear about how your discussion develops, stage by stage, as you work through the issues at hand.

Poor essay structure is one of the most common weaknesses in student essays, revealing a lack of skills such as clarity in arranging your thoughts for presentation to others. Therefore, you should avoid the 'domino' method of essay writing, whereby you write one sentence, then another one which seems to follow that one, then another one that seems to fit after the previous one, and so on until the requisite number of words is completed.

3.2 The essential components

The essential components of an essay written on one author or upon a theme linking many authors are now given.

3.2.1 The cover page

The cover page bears the name of the academic institution, the essay title, the professor's name, the student's name, the date and the place. The title should be brief and pithy, in other words precise and crisp. Generally one is wise to leave devising the exact title until the final form of the work has been written.

Example A

PONTIFICAL GREGORIAN UNIVERSITY

Faculty of Theology

TITLE OF ESSAY

Name of Professor
Course title

Name of student
Matriculation number

Place, Year

Example B

TERESIANUM

PONTIFICIO ISTITUTO DI SPIRITUALITÀ

TITLE OF ESSAY
Subtitle

Paper written for the course named X
Course serial number
Professor

Student: signature
Name e Surname
Matriculation N°:

Rome, Year

3.2.2 *The table of abbreviations*

The table of abbreviations should be devised as in the example below. Clearly, an abbreviation is italicized if it refers to a book title and not italicized if it refers to an author or an institution.

A

AAS	*Acta Apostolicae Sedis. Commentarium officiale.* Typis Polyglottis Vaticanis, 1909–
AASOR	*Annual of American Schools of Oriental Research*
AB	*Anchor Bible*
ABR	*Australian Biblical Review*
ADAJ	*Annual of the Department of Antiquities of Jordan*
AGJU	*Arbeiten zur Geschichte des antiken Judentums und des Urchristentums*
AGSU	*Arbeiten zur Geschichte des Spätjudentums und Urchristentums*
AJSL	*American Journal of Semitic Languages and Literature*
AJT	*Asia Journal of Theology*
ALGHJ	*Arbeitum zur Literatur und Geschichte des hellenistchen Judentums*
AnBib	*Analecta Biblica*
ANET	*Ancient Near Eastern Texts,* 3rd edition, James B. Pritchard, ed. (Princeton: 1969).
ANRW	*Aufsticg und Niedergang der römischen Welt*
ASNU	*Acta Seminarii Neotestamentici Upsaliensis*
ASOR	*American Schools of Oriental Research*
ASTI	*Annual of the Swedish Theological Institute*
ATANT	*Abhandlungen zur Theologie des Alten und Neuen Testaments*
ATD	*Das Alte Testament Deutsch*
ATR	*Anglican Theological Review*
AUSS	*Andrews University Seminary Studies*

B

BA	*Biblical Archaeologist*
BAR	*Biblical Archaeology Review*
BASOR	*Bulletin of the American Schools of Oriental Research*
BAT	*Botschaft des Alten Testaments*
BBB	*Bonner biblische Beiträge*
BBR	*Bulletin for Biblical Research*
BETL	*Bibliotheca Ephemeridum Theologicarum Lovaniensium*
BETS	*Bulletin of the Evangelical Theological Society*
BFCT	*Beiträge zur Förderung christlicher Theologie*
BGBE	*Beiträge zur Geschichre der biblischen Exegese*
BHS	*Biblia Hebraica Stuttgartensia*
BI	*Biblical Interpretation*
Bib	*Biblica*
Bib Tod	*Bible Today*
BiberOr	*Biblica et Orientalia. Rome: Biblical Institute Press.*
BibRev	*Bible Review*
BibThBul	*Biblical Theology Bulletin*
BibTod	*Bible Today*
BJRL	*Bulletin of the John Rylands Library*
BJS	*Brown Judaic Studies*
BKAT	*Biblischer Kommentar: Altes Testament*
BL	*Bampton Lectures*
BN	*Biblische Notizen*
BR	*Biblical Research*
BS	*Bibliotheca Sacra*
BSC	*Bible Student's Commentary*
BSNTS	*Bulletin of the Studiorum Novi Testamenti Societas*
BST	*Basel Studies in Theology*
BST	*Bible Speaks Today*
BTB	*Biblical Theological Bulletin*
BWANT	*Beitrage zur Wissenschaft vom Alten und Neuen Testament*

BU	*Biblische Untersuchungen*
BZ	*Biblische Zeitschrift*
BZAW	*Beihefte zur Zeitschrift für die alttestamentliche Wissenschaft*
BZNW	*Beihefte zur Zeitschrift für die neutestamentliche Wissenschaft*

C

CAT	*Commentaire de l'Ancien Testament*
CBC	*Cambridge Bible Commentary*
CBQ	*Catholic Biblical Quarterly*
CBQMS	*Catholic Biblical Quarterly Monograph Series*
CC	*Communicators Commentary*
CCC	*Catechism of the Catholic Church*
CCL	*Corpus Christianorum series latina.* Tournai: Brepols, 1954– .
CEB	*Commentaire Evangélique de la Bible*
CGSTJ	*China Graduate School if Theology Journal*
CIL	*Corpus Inscriptionum Latinarum*
CJT	*Canadian Journal of Theology*
CPh	*Classical philology*
CSEL	*Corpus Scriptorum Ecclesiasticorum Latinorum.* Wien: 1866– .
CSR	*Christian Scholar's Review*
CTJ	*Calvin Theological Journal*
CTM	*Concordia Theological Monthly*
CTR	*Criswell Theological Review*
CurTM	*Currents in Theology and Missions*

D

DOTT	*Documents of Old Testament Times.* D. Winton Thomas (ed.), New York: Harper & Row, 1958.
DP	*Discourses of the Popes from Pius XI to John Paul II to the Pontifical Academy of Sciences. 1936–1986.* Vatican City: Pontifical Academy of Sciences, 1986.

DR	*Downside Review*
DS	H. Denzinger and H. Schönmetzer. *Enchiridion Symbolorum, Definitionum et Declarationum de rebus fidei et morum.* Barcelona/Freiburg im Breisgau/Rome: Herder, 1976.
DSB	*Daily Study Bible*

E

EB	*Études Bibliques*
EBC	*Expositor's Bible Commentary*
EJ	*Evangelical Journal*
EJT	*European Journal of Theology*
EphTL	*Ephemerides Théologiques et Lovanienses*
EQ	*Evangelical Quarterly*
EstBib	*Estudios biblicos*
ETL	*Ephemerides Theologicae Lovanienses*
ETRel	*Études Théologiques et Religieuses*
EV	*Enchiridion Vaticanum.* Documenti ufficiali della Chiesa. Bologna: Edizioni Dehoniane.
EvT	*Evangelische Theologie*
Exp	*The Expositor*
ExpT	*Expository Times*

F

FCI	*Foundation of Evangelical Interpretation Series*
FOTL	*Forms of Old Testament Literature Series*
FRLANT	*Forschungen zur Religion und Literatur des Alten und Neuen Testaments*
FTS	*Frankfurter Theologische Studien*

G

GTJ	*Grace Theological Journal*
GRBS	*Greek, Roman and Byzantine Studies*

H

HAR	*Hebrew Annual Review*

HAT	*Handbuch zum Alten Testament*
HBT	*Horizons in Biblical Theology*
Herm	*Hermathena*
HJ	*Heythrop Journal*
HS	*Hebrew Studies*
HSMS	*Harvard Semitic Monograph Series*
HTR	*Harvard Theological Review*
HTS	*Harvard Theological Studies*
HUCA	*Hebrew Union College Annual*

I

IB	*Interpreter's Bible*
IBS	*Irish Biblical Studies*
ICC	*International Critical Commentary*
ICS	*Illinois Classical Studies*
IDB	*Interpreter's Dictionary of the Bible*
IDBS	*Interpreter's Dictionary of the Bible Supplement series*
IEJ	*Israel Exploration Journal*
Int	*Interpretation*
IG	*Insegnamenti di Giovanni Paolo II*. Vatican City: Vatican Polyglot Press, 1978–
ISBE	*International Standard Bible Encyclopedia, revised*
ITC	*International Theological Commentary*
ITQ	*Irish Theological Quarterly*

J

JAAR	*Journal of the American Academy of Religion*
JAOS	*Journal of the American Oriental Society*
JBL	*Journal of Biblical Literature*
JBLDS	*Journal of Biblical Literature Dissertation Series*
JBLMS	*Journal of Biblical Literature Monograph Series*
JBR	*Journal of the Bible and Religion*
JECS	*Journal of Early Christian Studies*
JETS	*Journal of the Evangelical Theological Society*
JJS	*Journal of Jewish Studies*

JNES	*Journal of Near Eastern Studies*
JNSL	*Journal of North West Semitic Languages*
JQR	*Jewish Quarterly Review*
JPS	Jewish Publication Society
JR	*Journal of Religion*
JSJ	*Journal for the Study of Judaism*
JSNT	*Journal for the Study of the New Testament*
JSNTSS	*Journal for the Study of the New Testament Supplement Series*
JSOT	*Journal for the Study of the Old Testament*
JSOTSS	*Journal for the Study of the Old Testament Supplement Series*
JSS	*Journal of Semitic Studies*
JTC	*Journal for Theology and the Church*
JTS	*Journal of Theological Studies*
JTSA	*Journal of Theology for Southern Africa*

K

KAT	*Kommentar zum Alten Testament*

L

LD	*Lecta Divina*
LouvStud	*Louvain Studies*
LThK	*Lexikon für Theologie und Kirche*
LXX	The Septuagint

M

MC	*The Modern Churchman*
MGWJ	*Monatsschrift für Geschichte und Wissenschaft des Judentums*
MT	Masoretic Text

N

ND	J. Neuner and J. Dupuis, *The Christian Faith in the Doctrinal Documents of the Catholic Church.* London: Collins, 1983.

Neot	*Neotestamentica*
NESTTR	*Near East School of Theology Theological Review*
NGTT	*Nederduits Gereformeerde Teologiese Tydskrif*
NICNT	*New International Commentary on the New Testament*
NICOT	*New International Commentary on the Old Testament*
NIDOTT	*New International Dictionary of Old Testament Theology*
NIGTC	*New International Greek Testament Commentary*
NovT	*Novum Testamentum*
NovTSup	*Novum Testamentum Supplements*
NTS	*New Testament Studies*
NTT	*Nederlands Theologisch Tijdschrift*

O

OR	*L'Osservatore Romano,* daily Italian edition
ORE	*L'Osservatore Romano,* weekly English edition
Ost	*Ostkirchliche Studien*
OTL	*Old Testament Library Commentary Series*
OTM	*Old Testament Message Series*
OTS	*Oudtestamentische Studiën*
OTSWA	*Oud Testamentaise Werkgemeenschap in Suid-Afrika*

P

PEQ	*Palestine Exploration Quarterly*
PG	J. P. Migne. *Patrologiae cursus completus, series graeca.* 161 vols. Paris: 1857–1866.
PL	J. P. Migne. *Patrologiae cursus completus, series latina.* 221 vols. Paris: 1844–1864.
PRS	*Perspectives on Religious Studies*
PTR	*Princeton Theological Review*

Q

R

RB	*Révue Biblique*
RBen	*Revue Benedictine*

RBPh	*Revue belge de philologie et d'histoire*
RdQ	*Revue de Qumran*
RefRev	*Reformed Review*
RelSRev	*Religious Studies Review*
ResQ	*Restoration Quarterly*
RevExp	*Review and Expositor*
RHPR	*Revue d'histoire et de philosophie religieuses*
RivBib	*Rivista Biblica*
RSR	*Recherches de science religieuse*
RTP	*Review of Theology and Philosophy*
RTR	*Reformed Theological Review*
RvExp	*Review and Expositor*

S

SBLDS	Society for Biblical Literature Dissertation Series
SBLMS	*Society for Biblical Literature Monograph Series*
SBLSP	*Society for Biblical Literature Seminar Papers*
SBT	*Studies in Biblical Theology*
SC	*Sources Chrétiennes*. Paris: Cerf, 1942– .
SCO	*Studi classici e orientali*
ScriptPhil	*Scripta Philosophica*
ScriptTheol	*Scripta Theologica*
SE	*Studia Evangelica*
SEÅ	*Svensk Exegetisk Årsbok*
SJLA	*Studies in Judaism in Late Antiquity*
SJOT	*Scandinavian Journal of the Old Testament*
SJT	*Scottish Journal of Theology*
SN	*Studia Neotestamentica*
SNTSMS	*Society of New Testament Studies Monograph Series*
SNTU	*Studien zum Neuen Testament und seiner Umwelt*
SR	*Studies in Religion*
SSN	*Studia semitica Neerlandica*
ST	*Studia Theologica*
StudBT	*Studia Biblica et Theologica*

StVTQ	*Saint Vladimir's Theological Quarterly*
SWJT	*Southwestern Journal of Theology*

T

TB	*Tyndale Bulletin*
TBC	*Torch Bible Commentaries*
TDNT	*Theological Dictionary of the New Testament*
TDOT	*Theological Dictionary of the Old Testament*
ThR	*Theologische Rundschau*
TLZ	*Theologische Literaturzeitung*
TNTC	*Tyndale New Testament Commentaries*
TOTC	*Tyndale Old Testament Commentaries*
TRev	*Theological Review*
TrinJ	*Trinity Journal*
TS	*Theological Studies*
TSK	*Theologische Studien und Kritiken*
TU	*Texte und Untersuchungen*
TynB	*Tyndale Bulletin*
TZ	*Theologische Zeitschrift*

U

USQR	*Union Seminary Quarterly Review*

V

VC	*Vigiliae Christianae*
VetChr	*Vetera Christianorum*
VT	*Vetus Testamentum*
VTSup	*Vetus Testamentum Supplements*

W

WBC	*Word Biblical Commentary*
WMANT	*Wissenschaftliche Monographien zum Alten und Neuen Testaments*
WUNT	*Wissenschaftliche Untersuchungen zum Neuen Testament*

XYZ

YNER	*Yale Near Eastern Researches*
ZAC	*Zeitschrift für Antikes Christentum*
ZAW	*Zeitschrift für die Alttestamentliche Wissenschaft*
ZDMG	*Zeitschrift der Deutschen Morganländischen Gesellschaft*
ZKG	*Zeitschrift für Kirchengeschichte*
ZNW	*Zeitschrift für die neutesamentliche Wissenschaft*
ZTK	*Zeitschrift für Theologie und Kirche*

After the table of abbreviations, a statement of the following kind can be made:

> The Scriptural quotations and abbreviations in this work are from the New Jerusalem Bible.

This statement implies that, generally, a consistent use is made of one version of the Bible throughout the work. It can safely be assumed that standard abbreviations like those in the following table need not be listed in your work.

Abbreviation	Meaning
app.	appendix
art.	article
chap.	chapter
div.	division
ed.	editor, edited by, edition
eds.	editors
et al.	and others (Latin *et alia*)
f. or ff.	folio(s)
ibid.	in the same place
Idem	the same
n.d.	no date
no. or nos.	number(s)

Abbreviation	Meaning
n.p.	no place
p. pp.	page(s)
par.	paragraph
pt.	part
rev.	revised
sec.	section
ser.	series
suppl.	supplement
s.v.	under the word (Latin *sub verso*)
tr.	translator(s)
vol.	volume

3.2.3 *The table of contents*

The table of contents serves as a schematic summary of the work.

3.2.4 *The introduction*

The introduction gives data about the author(s) studied along with a brief explanation of the background, as well as the limits and main sources used. It is often a wise decision to begin work on the introduction after you have completed a rough draft of the body of your paper. Many find the task of writing an introduction perplexing, wondering why they should write something if they are planning to say it again in the next paragraphs. After all, novels do not have ponderous opening paragraphs which explain what is going to happen in advance. However, the introduction is not a disposable redundancy; it is a crucial component of the essay.

An essay is an exploration of an idea which needs to be defined before it is developed. Because the material in an essay always relates to this central thesis, it is necessary for the writer to introduce that thesis and make the reader aware of its importance and relevance. The introduction is the place where the essay has to forge a good impression, informing the reader what is to come and encouraging him or her to read further (but without rendering the succeeding paragraphs repetitious). If the introduction is tedious or fails to make the rest of the essay sound interesting, the reader will not wish to continue.

Of course, when you are writing a class assignment, you can assume it will be read no matter how bad the introduction. However, your introduction serves the same purpose as it would if the reader were coming to it voluntarily. You must give the impression that your essay is worth reading. The introduction should be brief relative to the rest of the essay. If the opening is inappropriately lengthy, the reader will lose interest, annoyed that you have failed to get started. Do not include unnecessary background information, especially if your tutor is already conversant with the material on which you are writing.

In your introduction, first present the issues the essay is concerned with. In doing so, try to state briefly just what the question is and why it is a question. Next, explain how you are going to develop the question in the central body of the essay. This is usually done by giving a brief sketch or overview of the main points you will present, an overture, so to speak, of your essay's structure. This is one way of showing your reader that you have a grasp (and it also helps you get a grasp) of your essay as a structured and integrated whole, and gives some idea of what can be expected from the essay.

3.2.5 The central body

In the main body of your essay, you should do what you've promised. Here you should present your exposition and your critical discussion. Thus, it is here that the main meat of your topic is to be found. Of course, what that meat is and how you will serve it will depend on the particular topic before you. However, whatever the topic, make clear at each stage just what it is you are doing. You can be quite explicit about this.

Example

> I shall now outline Descartes' ontological argument for the existence of God, as it is presented in his Fifth Meditation. There will be three stages to this exposition.

Don't imagine that this explicitness must be too bland or the sign of an unsophisticated thinker. The old saying 'If you can't say what you mean, then you can't mean what you say' very much applies to writing an essay. This means that fine writing requires a good grasp of the language in which it is written, including the grammar and vocabulary.

Having a mastery of a good range of terms, being sensitive to the subtleties of their meaning, and being able to construct grammatically correct and properly punctuated sentences are essential to the clear articulation and development of your thoughts. Think of grammar, not as some old-fashioned set of rules of linguistic etiquette, but rather as the internal logic of a sentence, that is, as the relationships between the words within a sentence which enable them to combine to make sense. It's no good cementing your bricks together well if the bricks themselves crumble; and it's no good having solidly made bricks if your cement can't hold them together. Pay careful attention, then, to each and every sentence you write so that its sense is clear and is the sense you really intend it to have. Think carefully about what it is you want each particular sentence to do (in relation to both those sentences immediately surrounding it and the essay as a whole) and structure your sentence so that it does what you want it to do.

Good punctuation of a sentence should help to display its grammar. When reading your authors, attend closely to their sentence construction so as to be aware of all the subtleties of the text. Use your time at university to develop these skills further. It will be assumed that you can spell—which is not a matter of pressing the 'spell-check' key on a word-processor. A good dictionary and a thesaurus should always be within reach as you write your essay.

If you are concerned to write not only clearly and precisely, but also with some degree of grace and style, it's still best to get the clarity and precision correct first, in a plain, straightforward way, and then to polish things up afterwards to acquire the style and grace. Don't sacrifice clarity and precision for the sake of style and grace—be prepared to sacrifice that beautiful turn of phrase if its presence is going to send your discussion off down an awkward path of reasoning. Aim to hit the nail on the head, rather than make a loud bang. What you are likely to find, nonetheless, is that an essay which really is clear and precise will have a large measure of grace and style in its very clarity and precision.

The need for clarity and precision in essay writing sometimes means that you need to stipulate your own meaning for a term. When you want to use a particular word in a special way for the purposes of your essay—as a technical term—be clear about it.

Example

> In this essay, I shall intend 'eros' to mean the desire for wholeness.

Also, be consistent in your technical meanings, or else note when you are not. Be wary, though, of inventing too many neologisms or being too idiosyncratic in your stipulations.

Certain items are to be avoided at all costs in the essay. Among these are padding, waffle, vagueness, ambiguity, abbreviations and colloquialisms. Other elements which are not welcome in an essay are: writing whose syntax merely reflects the patterns of speech; unnecessary abstractness or indirectness; unexplained jargon; overly-rhetorical questions and other flourishes. Also, try to shorten and simplify sentences where you can do so without sacrificing the subtlety and inherent complexity of your thinking. Avoid thinking that obscurity is a sign of profundity. Nonetheless, don't be afraid of sometimes saying things which happen to sound a little odd, if you think you have expressed your ideas just as they should be expressed. In expounding a text or problem that ultimately is just vague, muddled, or obscure, try to convey such vagueness, muddle or obscurity clearly, rather than simply reproducing it in your own writing. That is, be clear when and how a text or problem has such features, and then perhaps do your best to make matters clearer.

The central body of the text has headings which order the distribution of the material. The decimal method of division indicated below in chapter four (§4.5.9) for theses, is useful. Each heading should be short and to the point. Diagrams should be used in the text only if they serve a real purpose.

3.2.6 *The conclusion*

The conclusion sums up the main point of the work, and this can often be the hardest part of the essay, especially if you are not exactly sure what you have said. If you have had your topic in view throughout the essay, you should be able to announce a specific conclusion confidently and definitely. If you cannot find a way to sum up what you have said, then you have not said anything.

What you say in your conclusion should match what you said when you introduced the essay: it should be a restatement (but not a mere repetition) of your thesis, ideally in a way that shows more fully and clearly what you have been arguing. If the process of writing the essay has changed what you are arguing—and this is surprisingly often the case—you may have to reword your proposal in the introduction. Otherwise, the essay will suffer from schizophrenia.

In the conclusion, begin by retracing the steps of your argument. By doing so, you remind the reader of how the components of the essay fit together, and strengthen their cumulative effect. Because this part is a conclusion, you must be conclusive; that is, you must present your point in its final, most persuasive form. In the introduction you were giving the reader an idea of what was to follow, trying to attract interest. In the conclusion, you have the weight of the essay behind you, and you can state your case succinctly, knowing that the reader has all the information you have provided. The introduction is a forecast, while the conclusion is a final analysis. Avoid repeating the introduction too closely; the tone of your conclusion is different because the reader has finished your paper.

Once you have tied up your argument, a good way to conclude is to use the final lines of your essay to suggest a way in which the material you have covered applies to a larger concern. As in the introduction you explained the thesis in terms of a bigger picture, so in the conclusion you can demonstrate the effects or the problems inherent in what you have discussed. For example, a paper on ecology might end with a warning about the consequences of irresponsible practices. Remember, however, that an overly sentimental or obvious statement will weaken rather than strengthen your essay ('If we do not save the forests the entire world is at risk').

A typical way to impart a sense of unity to an essay is to return at the end to a quotation, image, or statement that the essay began with. Some people call this 'closing the circle'.[7] This technique, if carried out effectively, conveys a sense of order, elegance, and thought that can make a reader smile with appreciation. A seasoned writer doesn't merely repeat exactly what was said at the beginning; rather he or she echoes the words or image at the beginning, while adding some new twist or turn to deepen the perspective.

3.2.7 Citations

The essay should contain a number of citations from the author(s) studied. These citations should be referenced with either footnotes or end notes, indicating sources or giving further information on the text. Chapter five should be consulted for information on how to proceed in this respect. It important to reference your sources properly for three basic reasons. First, your tutors will be able to see evidence that you have done useful and relevant research for your assignment. They will be able to verify what sort of reading you are doing—are you just looking at the course books or are you reading around the topic? Second, as we've already said, if you don't reference your sources you could be guilty of plagiarism. Third, furnishing full details of your sources allows the reader to follow them up if they want to. It may be that the quotation you use from a particular book prompts the reader to want to go and find that specific book.

---

7. See, for example, M. Harvey, *The Nuts and Bolts of College Writing* (Indianapolis: Hackett, 2000).

3.2.8 The appendix

An appendix may be used if necessary.

3.2.9 The bibliography

The bibliography lists works employed during research, divided according to primary and secondary sources. Chapter six should be consulted for information on how to do this.

3.3 The final product

It is an illusion that the student will be able to write a perfect essay first time round. Normally, it will be more like the sculptor taking a block of rock and slowly carving it into shape. The writer must arrive via successive approximations at the final product. Before you can start writing your first draft you should have done three things: carried out all the necessary reading, made notes and also constructed an essay plan. You should have a fairly good idea of what you need and want to say. Now you are going to say it in the most effective way possible. The first draft is where you begin to express your ideas and organise your materials, putting them together under different section headings. It is where you sketch out the main points of your argument and illustrate them with examples. The writing is rough because you need to work through what you think, what your argument is, and what sources you are going to use at various stages. It is crucial to keep writing; this is only the first draft so it does not have to be perfect. The important thing is to produce a chunk or chunks of text you can work with and start to shape into the piece of work you will eventually hand in. Thinking about your first draft in these terms will help to make the writing process less stressful.

Once you have made your first draft, you can revise it to see that it matches your overall theme and that each section carries your argument forward. The first thing to do is print out your first draft, which offers a much better idea of what it looks like than the on-screen version. You need to ask if it seems like an essay or just like a collection of sentences and notes. The second thing worth doing is to read it out aloud to yourself. You need to ask if the essay makes sense, with sentences flowing properly. Does the essay stumble over short phrases or is it getting lost in sentences that go on for half a page? These forms of appraisal enable you to check the overall form of your essay.

Next, you should focus on the individual sections of your discussion. You should work through them systematically, rewriting them as necessary to make sure that each section is clear and contains all the relevant material. You will need to make sure that they are linked together and that your argument flows clearly and naturally. You should also start concentrating on style and checking for grammatical errors and typing mistakes. The second draft is a good time to use tutor feedback from your most recent essays.

Before you deliver your essay to your professor, be sure that it is visually satisfactory: look for careless mistakes. Proofreading is an essential task that many writers do not take seriously. Reread the essay, out loud if possible, to make sure that it flows well and that it makes sense as a whole. Since you have worked on the essay one section at a time, you may have forgotten to connect those sections properly. Reading your essay aloud from beginning to end may make you realize that it is less coherent or not as thorough as you had thought, and you may even have to do some last minute research to bolster a weak point. Hearing a sentence may make its faults clearer than they appear on the page. You may discover that you have left a sentence incomplete, omitted a citation, or (if you are using a computer) forgotten to erase unwanted text.

If you have used a word-processor, you must beware of the illusion of perfection that the printed page presents. Your essay looks so official and sophisticated that mistakes seem inconceivable. However, they are probably there. A typing mistake is no less an error than a spelling mistake. While the professor may know that the error comes from your fingers rather than your brain, the experience of reading your paper will still have been interrupted, and there will be an ugly gash of red ink on the page. One of the most efficient ways of picking up spelling errors is to read your work backwards, word for word. That way you are looking at each individual word, not reading for the overall sense of the passage. Alternatively, ask a friend to read your paper, or (best of all, both for spelling and for style) leave the paper for several days, then come back and read it carefully. The only problem with this last solution is that it is not often practical in the real world of university assignments and deadlines. The presentation of your essay is not a trivial matter; you wish to show the reader that you are thorough and organized. A series of mistakes suggests that you are careless, and does not reflect well upon your work. Check very carefully for errors in spelling, typing, and, especially in the Bibliography, punctuation. Most examiners deduct marks for these mistakes.

4 THE THESIS

True ease in writing comes from art, not chance,
As those move easiest who have learned to dance.

Alexander Pope, *Essay on Criticism*

The last thing one discovers in writing a book is what to put first.

Blaise Pascal, *Pensées*

4.1 The choice of theme

The first phase is one of reflection and mulling over possible research projects. Usually the early phases of a graduate program proceed in clear and very structured ways. One day, however, the clear structure begins to diminish and now you're approaching the thesis or dissertation stage. This is a new and exciting time. These next steps are more and more defined by you and not your supervisor, the program, or the department. First, be inclusive with your thinking. Don't try to eliminate ideas too quickly. Build on your ideas and see how many different research projects you can identify. Give yourself the luxury of being expansive in your thinking at this stage—you won't be able to do this later on: try and be creative. As you reflect, write down your ideas. This will allow you to revisit an idea later on. Or, you can modify and change an idea. If you don't write down your ideas, they tend to be in a continual state of flux and you will probably have the feeling that you're not going anywhere. What a great feeling it is to be able to sit down and scan the many ideas you have been thinking about, if they're written down! Try not to be overly influenced at this time by what you feel others expect from you (your colleagues, your profession, your academic department, and so forth). You have a much better chance of selecting a topic that will be really of interest to you if it is *your* topic. This will be one of the few opportunities you may have in your professional life to focus in on a research topic that is really of your own choosing. Don't begin your thinking by assuming that your research will draw international attention to you. Instead, be realistic in setting your goal. Make sure your expectations are tempered by:

1. the realization that you are fulfilling an academic requirement;
2. the fact that the process of conducting the research may be just as important (or more important) as the outcomes of the research;
3. the idea that first and foremost the whole research project should be a learning experience for you.

If you can keep these ideas in mind while you're thinking through your research, you stand an excellent chance of having your research project turn out well.

Be realistic about the time that you are willing to commit to your research project. If it's a five year project that you're thinking about, admit it at the beginning and then decide whether or not you have five years to give to it. If the project you'd like to do is going to demand more time than you're willing to commit then you have a problem.

4.1.1 Field of interest

The next stage is to formulate your theme. Clearly, the topic must lie within the general area of interest of the faculty in which the work is being carried out. If the faculty is Theology, then the topic should have a mainly theological slant. Similar considerations apply with Philosophy, Scripture, Canon Law, Bioethics, Ecclesiastical History, Spirituality, Patristics, Psychology, Social Sciences and so on. Interdisciplinary activity can be undertaken, but within well-defined parameters, otherwise the result is a vague piece of written work. In the search for a theme, one may begin from personal interest or from concrete and specific pastoral or missionary situations or else from scholarly discussions.

Ensure your proposal has a comprehensive review of the literature included. Many students feel that at the proposal stage it is not necessary or even desirable to do a complete literature search for the dissertation. The rationale behind an early literature review consists of an argument with two lines of analysis: first, this research is actually needed, and second the methodology you have chosen is most appropriate for the question that is being asked. Now is the time to get informed and to learn from others who have preceded you! If you wait until you are writing the dissertation it is too late. It is always possible to add to the body of literature when you're writing the final dissertation.

With the ready availability of photocopy machines and scanners you have a useful tool to collect material. When you read something that is important to your study, photocopy or scan the relevant article or section. Keep your photocopies organized according to categories and sections. And, most importantly, photocopy the bibliographic citation so that you can easily reference the material in your bibliography. Then, when you decide to sit down and actually write the literature review, bring out your photocopied sections, put them into logical and sequential order, and begin your writing.

4.1.2 Specific nature

A good proposal should consist of the first three chapters of the dissertation. It should begin with a statement of the background (*status quaestionis*) of the study (typically chapter 1 of the dissertation), then move on to a review of the literature (chapter 2), and conclude with a defining of the research methodology (chapter 3). Focus your research very specifically. Don't try to have your research cover too broad an area, even if you think that this will distort what you want to do. This may be the case, but you will be able to do the project only if it is narrowly defined. Usually a broadly defined project is not feasible. By defining too broadly it may sound better to you, but there is a great chance that it will be unmanageable as a research project. When you complete your research project it is important that you have something specific and definitive to contribute. This can be assisted and enhanced by narrowly defining your project. Otherwise you may have only broadly based ideas to offer about large areas that really provide little guidance to others that may follow you. Often the researcher finds that what he or she originally thought to be a good research project really turns out to be a group of research projects. Do one project for your dissertation and save the other projects for later in your career. Don't try to solve all of the problems in this one research project.

Include a title on your proposal. A good proposal has a good title and it is the first thing to help the reader begin to understand the nature of your work. Work on your title early in the process and revisit it often, in order to refine it. It's easy for a reader to identify those proposals where the title has been focused upon by the student. Preparing a good title means:

1. having the most important words appear toward the beginning of your title;

2. limiting the use of ambiguous or confusing words;
3. breaking up your title into a title and subtitle when you have too many words, and including key words that will help future researchers find your work.

It's important that your research proposal be organized around a set of questions that will guide your study. When selecting these guiding questions try to write them so that they frame your research and put it into perspective with other studies. These questions must serve to establish the link between your research and other work that has preceded you. Your research questions should clearly show the relationship of your investigation to your field of study. Don't be carried away at this point and make your questions too narrow. You must start with broad relational questions.

A thesis has a specific nature, which differs from that of a book, a lecture-course or a meditation. It is an exercise based on scientific research. Therefore, the theme should be restricted to a *limited* field which is precise in its scope. This must be borne in mind right from the start, so as to avoid the danger of not being able to explain the theme fully or else of falling into the trap of superficiality.

4.1.3 Scientific research

The thesis is based on scientific research, and it is not a meditation. Nevertheless, this does not exclude some degree of inspiration, reflection and personal interest. A thesis requires to be accompanied by a good bibliography indicating sound sources and documents. However attractive a theme may be, it would be unwise to pursue it if there is insufficient material. Often personal interest in a theme must be balanced against the practicality of being able to carry it out. It is also necessary to weigh up whether there is sufficient material in the language in which the thesis will be written; otherwise, it will be necessary to translate large quantities of material, which is very time-consuming.

4.1.4 Different types of theses

The difference between a Master's thesis (or Licentiate thesis) and a doctoral thesis should be borne in mind. Most universities stipulate a minimum and maximum length for a thesis. For a Master's or Licentiate thesis the length is usually around 50–100 pages of double-spaced A4 sheets. For doctorates, at many universities the recommended length is often 200–300 pages of double-spaced A4 sheets. A careful check should be made to see whether the recommended length at the particular place of learning includes or excludes references and bibliography. The purpose of a Master's (or Licentiate) thesis is not the presentation of an original piece of work. Rather it is an exercise in the skills of research, in the use and organization of sources, and in the employment of a consistent form of methodology for citing sources and constructing a bibliography. In this sense, it is a preparation for a doctoral thesis. On the other hand, the doctoral dissertation involves in-depth investigation on one precise area, in such a way as to be a contribution to greater understanding in that field. The originality may consist in investigation of a new area, or a new look at an old question, or a panoramic view of a particular field taking a critical look at recent developments.

4.2 Starting research

4.2.1 The plan

At the beginning, it is advisable to have a provisional plan which serves to give direction to the research. This plan should have two characteristics:

1. It should be a simple guide and should combine intuitive and organisational aspects. Don't impose an order, but rather evoke it.
2. It is provisional, in that it will be progressively modified and deepened as the research proceeds. Thus it is almost always necessary to adapt the plan as the work continues. Be flexible within a structure.

4.2.2 The sources

It is important to know how to read the sources in order to seek and note the various possible relations of the text with the chosen theme. In this way the various facets of the theme are explored. Primary sources are always preferable to secondary ones, since they furnish first-hand testimony or direct evidence concerning the topic under investigation. The question which must be asked is: how does the text illustrate the particular chosen theme? At the same time the thought of another author must not be forced so as to fit into the pre-determined scheme of the thesis. It is sometimes useful if one particular work (or series of works) lies at the heart of the inspiration of a thesis, but this kind of book is not always easy to find. In such a case, the student must scrupulously avoid simply merely copying the thought of the basic work. Rather, it is necessary to read the basic work many times so as to understand how some of its ideas may be woven into the thread of the thesis.

4.2.3 *Reflecting*

Of all the various stages in writing a thesis, namely collecting material, organizing the material, reflecting upon the material thus organized and collected, writing and re-writing, perhaps the most underestimated phase is that of *reflecting*. At this stage, nothing appears to happen, but like a seed buried deep in the earth, ideas are germinating. The work is like fine wine that is maturing. One friend even advised me to have a pen and paper ready at my bedside in case ideas occurred to me in the middle of the night!

4.2.4 *Making notes*

During the reading process, it is important to have an effective way of making notes. One way is the use of index-cards which was described in chapter one, sub-section 1.3.4. Here are some further hints on making notes using index cards:

1. The whole text should not be copied, but only those ideas or expressions which are particularly relevant to the theme. You need to distinguish the essential from the incidental. It is necessary to understand the thought of the author, and to summarize that thought.
2. Only one main idea should be put on each index-card. An attempt should be made to cross reference ideas on the various index cards, so as to build up a relationship between them.
3. Complete bibliographical references should be taken for each text that is copied. This includes the surname and initial(s) of authors, full titles of books and articles, names and locations of publishing houses, publication dates and full parameters of journals consulted. It is better to copy down too much concerning these parameters than too lit-

tle. Often students and scholars have to return to sources at a later stage because of omissions earlier on; this is time-consuming as well as frustrating.

4. Personal reflections should be added on what is read, namely those reactions which the text inspires in the student. These ideas will often serve as a basis in the writing of the thesis.

4.3 Precise theme and plan

4.3.1 Mutual link between the theme and the plan

There is a mutual relation between clarifying the theme and formulating the plan. Sometimes it is necessary to reformulate the theme to express the content more faithfully; however, it is also necessary to arrange the content so that it follows the theme. It should be borne in mind that in many universities, provisional approval of a theme is given at the very start of research and then more definite approval once work has got under way and there is a solid chance of success. A theme which has been approved provisionally as an indication of a field of research can be reformulated or further specified according to the results of the research undertaken. The title of a thesis may even need slight modification as the research matures.

4.3.2 Characteristics of the plan

Since the thesis must be a single unit, the plan must follow a dynamic and logical progression. Each chapter must be relevant to the overall theme, and each chapter must lead logically into the next one.

In order to develop the plan in this way, it is necessary to ask the questions: What do I intend to explain? What is the basic thought or key idea that I wish to expound? The thesis must then be shaped around this key idea.

A suitable division of chapters should be ensured. It should be kept in mind that in a Master's thesis of say 80 pages, 5 pages will go to the introduction and 5 to the conclusion. Then, a division could be made into three chapters of about 20 pages each or four chapters of about 15 pages. Each chapter of a thesis should contain *roughly* the same amount of material and thus each should be of similar length. The plan, if efficiently made according to the order of the work, will then help greatly in dividing up the text.

4.4 *Writing*

A frequent problem writing a thesis is feeling blocked, and writers who sit around waiting for inspiration tend to put off writing. Writer's block is a temporary or lasting failure to put words on paper. It can hit every writer, if only for a few minutes or a day or two, but it becomes a real problem when the writer is not reaching targets and when they feel incapable of completing a piece of work. Professional writers make sure they are inspired at a set time every morning, following Pliny the Elder's adage, '*Nulla dies sine linea*', which loosely rendered means 'don't let a day go by without writing something'.[1] One must be able to write without being inspired. That's the difference between a professional and an amateur. A professional cook can prepare a good meal even when not inspired! During the writing process, it is important to stay motivated and to stay sane. This may mean taking breaks, doing other things, and leaving your work to rest and mature. This is different from writer's block, because the process is still continuing albeit in a more passive way. There is thus a difference between a good

1. Pliny the Elder, *Naturalis historia*, 35.

writing discipline where sometimes you write, even when you don't feel like it, and forcing yourself to write when you really should avoid it, since you are over tired.

The first step is to move from planning and note taking to a written prose text. Don't wait for a perfect formulation; you will need to proceed through at least three successive approximations or drafts before arriving at the final text. It is better to rapidly formulate a first draft with all its imperfections, and then polish it up, rather than try to write as perfectly as possible first time around. The adage that 'the art of writing is rewriting', should be borne in mind.[2] Perfectionism should be avoided in a thesis which is an exercise, rather than a faultless finished product. An imperfect finished thesis is preferable to a hypothetically perfect work which is never completed.

For some students the fact that writing a thesis is a long-term commitment can be a problem. The immediate goal may not be in sight for many months or even a couple of years. Rather like the climber tackling a high and arduous mountain, the student may feel a type of vertigo or even discouragement that things are not going quicker or more successfully. Up till now, he or she has written shorter essays and has been able to see the results rapidly. For this reason, writing a long thesis, at doctoral level, is often preceded by an 'apprenticeship' where the student writes a short work (at Master's level) which can serve as a test to establish whether the student is capable, psychologically as well as academically, of assuming the

2. See R. N. Patterson: 'Writing is rewriting. A writer must learn to deepen characters, trim writing, intensify scenes. To fall in love with the first draft to the point where one cannot change it is to greatly enhance the prospects of never publishing.' Harry Shaw, in *Errors in English and Ways to Correct Them*, observes: 'There is no such thing as good writing. There is only good rewriting.' Science fiction novelist Michael Crichton agrees: 'Books are not written—they're rewritten.'

responsibility for a longer and more demanding piece of writing. Also, most doctoral programs have a mechanism whereby, at a relatively early stage after enrolment, the student requires approval of his or her work, before much time and effort are invested in the process.

The thesis supervisor is the person who should be able to offer support and encouragement to the student during the arduous period of writing. A thesis supervisor is usually a member of the faculty within the student's academic department or program. The selection of a supervisor should be based primarily upon competence in the field of the proposed thesis topic. Within this restriction, the department should seek to accommodate the student's choice of supervisor, although it is not obliged to guarantee the choice. Among the responsibilities of the thesis supervisor would be the following:

1. to provide reasonable access to students and to be available for consultation at relatively short notice;
2. to be as helpful as possible in suggesting research topics and in assisting students to define their theses;
3. to tell students approximately how long it will be before written work, such as drafts of chapters, can be returned with comments;
4. to be thorough in their examination of thesis chapters, supplying, where appropriate, detailed comments on such matters as literary form, structure, use of evidence, relation of the thesis to published work on the subject, footnoting, and bibliographical techniques, and making constructive suggestions for rewriting and improving the draft;
5. to indicate clearly when a draft is in a satisfactory final form or, if it is clear to the supervisor that the thesis cannot be successfully completed, to advise the student accordingly;

6. to know the departmental and University regulations and standards to which the writer of a thesis is required to conform, and to make sure that the student is aware of them;
7. to continue supervision when on leave, possibly with arrangements also being made for members of a supervisory committee to assist the student for the leave period.

It is wise to write the first chapter, then hand it to the thesis director, supervisor or moderator for comments. Then the same should be done with the second chapter and so on. You should only return to the first chapter at the end, because only at that point will you gain an overview of the whole work, and you will see more clearly what changes are needed. The moderator may also suggest another approach.

The difference between note taking and composition is that the former tends to be a mechanical, routine action whereas the latter is an inspired, creative act. A plan is simply a tool to help the thesis writer get moving on a first draft. The final structure should be chosen to help the reader. In between, there may be many changes and revisions. At the first draft stage, you don't yet know what will make it into the final version. Also you will not be concentrating on making references and bibliography. That means you don't have to stop your writing to check facts, get the quote right, complete the references. Your thesis must not simply consist of a collection of unconnected or unrelated papers published or otherwise. However, it may include publishable work provided it is part of a connected argument and is uniform in presentation and format with the remainder of the dissertation.

In the first draft, you start to express your ideas, organising them and putting them together under different section headings. The writing is rough because you need to work through what you think, what your argument is, what theoretical writing you are going to use, and what other sources may be employed. The second draft is based on your rough draft, which you revise to see that it matches your overall argument and topic and that each section carries your argument forward. You are looking at the overall shape of your work, checking that it makes sense and that the order of your discussion is clear and natural. The third draft focuses on the individual sections of your discussion. You will rewrite them as necessary making sure that each section is clear and contains all the relevant material. You will need to ensure that they are linked together and that your argument flows clearly and naturally. You should also concentrate on style and check for grammatical errors.

Remember that writing is always a form of communication, in which you're always addressing somebody. If thesis scholars are confident in the support of their immediate addressee—normally their supervisor—and if they have a certain freedom and leeway in their work, then they feel relatively safe addressing somebody, and this makes the writing process not only easier but more pleasurable. Indeed, there are two kinds of problem. One is when you don't feel at ease addressing somebody else, maybe because you are overawed by their apparently prodigious knowledge or their particular manner. The other problem is if you tend to address only yourself and your discourse becomes a kind of closed circuit. The ideal situation is where you can integrate what you should say as a duty and what you'd like to say because it's creative; not just what you feel you ought to say, but what you really want to say.

The originality in a thesis may not lie in its content; as one commentator cynically stated: 'The average Ph.D. thesis is nothing but the transference of bones from one graveyard to another.'[3] The original contribution may consist in a new way of looking at an old topic, a new way of organizing ideas which have already been proposed, or a new, further interpretation of existing results.

4.5 Thesis structure

This section furnishes details of the main components of a research thesis. Clearly some of the following items are common to all theses while others are optional.

4.5.1 Title page[4]

The title page should generally contain the following information:

1. the name of the university and the faculty;
2. the title of the thesis;
3. the name of the author;
4. the name of the supervisor or director of the thesis and sometimes the second readers according to the norms of the particular university;
5. the city and year of publication.

Here are some examples of title pages:

3. F. J. Dobie, *A Texan in England* (Boston: Little, Brown, 1945).
4. The title page of a book, thesis or other written work is the page at or near the front which displays its title, and author, as well as other information. This is no longer synonymous with frontispiece in modern usage. A frontispiece is a decorative illustration facing a book's title page. The frontispiece is the verso (left-hand page) opposite the recto title page.

A1. Licentiate thesis in Bioethics at the Pontifical Athenaeum Regina Apostolorum:

PONTIFICAL ATHENAEUM

REGINA APOSTOLORUM

THESIS FOR THE LICENTIATE IN BIOETHICS

A bioethical discussion
on the research and use of embryonic stem cells

by
Sr. Joan Smith

Director: Fr. John Brown

Rome, May 2003

A2. Licentiate thesis at the Pontifical Gregorian University:

PONTIFICAL GREGORIAN UNIVERSITY

Faculty of Theology

FAITH AND SCIENCE
SINCE
GAUDIUM ET SPES

Tesina for the Licentiate
in Fundamental Theology
presented to
Fr. Gerald O'Collins S.J.

by

Fr. Paul Haffner
Venerable English College

Rome, 22 February 1982

A3. Doctoral thesis in theology at the Pontifical Gregorian University:

PONTIFICIA UNIVERSITAS GREGORIANA

Facultas Theologiae

Fr. Paul Haffner

CHRISTIAN FAITH IN GOD THE CREATOR
IN RELATION TO MODERN SCIENCE
ACCORDING TO THE WORKS OF STANLEY L.
JAKI

Dissertatio ad Doctoratum

Moderator: R.P. Willibrord Welten, S.I.

Roma 1987

A4. Doctoral thesis in philosophy at the Pontifical Urban University

PONTIFICIA UNIVERSITAS URBANIANA

Facoltà di Filosofia

TITLE OF THESIS

Name of student

Tesi di Laurea in Filosofia

Moderatore: Professor..................................

Correlatori: 1. Professor................................
2. Professor................................

City

Year

A5. Doctoral thesis in Canon Law at the Angelicum University

PONTIFICIA STUDIORUM UNIVERSITATIS
S. THOMAE IN URBE

Facultas Iuris Canonici

Fred A. Jones

A NEW STUDY
CONCERNING FEAST DAYS
ACCORDING TO CANON 1246 §1
Historico-theological and canonical aspects

(Dissertatio ad Doctoratum)

Moderator: John G. Smith, O.P.

Roma 1991

4.5.2 *The abstract*

Where it is required, the abstract is a useful summary of the work, which is sometimes printed on the back cover of a published thesis. A good abstract explains in one line why the dissertation is important. It then goes on to give a summary of the major results. The final sentences explain the major implications of the work. A good abstract is concise, readable, and quantitative. The appropriate length should be around one or two paragraphs, or approximately 400 words. Abstracts generally do not carry citations, and information in titles should not be repeated. The answers to the following questions should be found in the abstract:

1. What did you do?
2. Why did you do it? What question were you trying to answer?
3. How did you do it? State the methods.
4. What did you learn? State the major results.
5. Why does it matter? Point out at least one significant implication.

4.5.3 *Table of Contents*

The table of contents lists all headings and subheadings of the thesis, with page numbers, and suitably indented subheadings.

4.5.4 *List of Figures*

The list of figures (where required) furnishes page numbers of all figures. The list should include a short title for each figure but not the whole caption.

4.5.5 List of Tables

The list of tables (where required) furnishes page numbers of all tables. The list should include a short title for each table but not the whole caption.

4.5.6 Preface

The preface is a personal beginning to the thesis, and would include thanks and acknowledgements. Among acknowledgements would feature thanks to the supervisor(s) and anyone who helped you technically (including materials, supplies), intellectually (with assistance, advice), financially (for example, departmental support, travel grants, benefactors) and spiritually (moral support, parents, religious superiors).

4.5.7 Table of Abbreviations

The principle is the same as for essays, outlined in chapter three, subsection 3.2.2.

4.5.8 Introduction

The introduction is the scientific beginning of the thesis and yet it is like the overture in a musical symphony. Centuries ago, St Thomas Aquinas offered an excellent piece of advice about introductions. Here, the author does three things, having three objects in view: first, to gain the reader's good will; second, to dispose him to learn; third, to win his attention. The first object is achieved by showing the reader the value of the knowledge in question; the second by explaining the plan and divisions of the treatise; the third by warning him of its difficulties.[5]

---

5. See St Thomas Aquinas, *Commentary on Aristotle's* De anima, Book I, Lectio 1, 2.

You cannot write a good introduction until you know what the body of the thesis says. Consider writing the introductory sections after you have completed the rest of the text, rather than before. Be sure to include a link at the beginning of the introduction. This is a statement of something sufficiently interesting to motivate your reader to read the rest of the book, it is an important anchor to interesting questions that your thesis either solves or addresses. You should draw the reader in and make them want to read the rest of the text. The next paragraphs in the introduction should cite previous research in the area. It should cite those who had the idea or ideas first, and should also cite those who have done the most recent and relevant work. You should then go on to explain why your work was then necessary, as further research. The essential components of the introduction include:

1. A statement of the goal of the thesis: why the study was undertaken, or why the text was written. This should not be a repetition of the abstract.
2. Sufficient background information to allow the reader to understand the context and significance of the question under consideration.
3. Appropriate acknowledgement of the previous work on which you are building. This should contain sufficient references to enable the reader to achieve a sophisticated understanding of the context and significance of the question.
4. The introduction should be focused on the thesis topic. All cited work should be directly relevant to the goals of the thesis. This is not a place to summarize everything you have ever read about the subject.
5. Explain the scope of your work, what will and will not be included.

6. A verbal road map should be furnished, guiding the reader to what lies ahead.
7. It should be obvious where introductory material ends and your own contribution begins.

4.5.9 The main body

Each of the various chapters should have a title which is short and encapsulates the content of the chapter in a pithy way. The decimal division is a useful method for subdividing chapters, and runs as follows:

Chapter 1
Section 1 is 1.1.
Subdivisions of this are 1.1.1, 1.1.2, 1.1.3 etc.
Section 2 is 1.2
Subdivisions of this are 1.2.1, 1.2.2, 1.2.3 etc.
Section 3 is 1.3
Subdivisions of this are 1.3.1, 1.3.2, 1.3.3 etc.
The same for other sections

Chapter 2
Section 1 is 2.1.
Subdivisions of this are 2.1.1, 2.1.2, 2.1.3 etc.
Section 2 is 2.2
Subdivisions of this are 2.2.1, 2.2.2, 2.2.3 etc.
Section 3 is 2.3
Subdivisions of this are 2.3.1, 2.3.2, 2.3.3 etc.
The same for other sections

Chapter 3
Section 1 is 3.1.
Subdivisions of this are 3.1.1, 3.1.2, 3.1.3 etc.
Section 2 is 3.2
Subdivisions of this are 3.2.1, 3.2.2, 3.2.3 etc.
Section 3 is 3.3
Subdivisions of this are 3.3.1, 3.3.2, 3.3.3 etc.
The same for other sections

The same principle is applied to each chapter; it is not necessary that each chapter have the same number of sections and sub-divisions.

It is important to ensure consistency in the process of numbering the pages of the thesis. The first two pages which are blank are counted for the purposes of page numbering, even though no number actually appears on them. The cover page also counts as two page numbers, even though no number actually appears on either side of it. The table of contents which then follows is numbered as either -5- or preferably -v-. Generally it is better to use Roman numerals for the front matter of the thesis. Thus the preface, foreword and abbreviations pages are numbered in Roman numerals. The text itself then begins in Arabic numerals at -1-. Each new chapter (and the bibliography, appendix and index) begins on a new odd-numbered page.

4.5.10 References

References should be made according to the principles listed in chapter five below.

4.5.11 Conclusion

The conclusion is the point to draw together the main threads of the work and state what has been gained from doing it. This part should answer the question: What is the strongest and most important statement that you can make from your work? Or else: If you met the reader at a meeting six months from now, what do you want them to remember about your paper? Refer back to the topic posed, and describe the conclusions that you reached from carrying out this investigation, and summarize new observations, new interpretations, and new insights that have resulted from the present work. Include the broader implications of your results. Do not repeat word for word the abstract or introduction or discussion.

4.5.12 *Appendix*

The appendix, if it is necessary, is the part to include specific unpublished material (such as letters) for the reader's benefit. Of course, permission must be obtained from the owner of the material to do this.

4.5.13 *Glossary*

A glossary of terms may sometimes be useful, if these expressions have not been explained in the notes.

4.5.14 *Bibliography*

The bibliography lists works employed during research, divided according to primary and secondary sources. A bibliography is constructed according to the guidelines offered in chapter six.

4.5.15 *Index*

This is a useful item for a doctorate thesis. Only the text proper with its references is indexed. Forewords, prefaces, and bibliographies are not taken into account. Generally it is an index of proper names that is required, as the subjects should be clearly delineated in the table of contents. However, it is possible to make an index of names and a separate index of subjects, or else a combined index. Consistency should be ensured in the use of alphabetical order as regards peoples' names; more on this can be seen in chapter six, subsection 6.1.1 below. For the construction of the index, either a word-processing program should be used or the following method, with a *copy* of the typescript.

1. On the duplicate manuscript are highlighted (e.g. by coloured underlining), right from the moment of writing the first chapter, the names or key words or phrases that are chosen for the index entries.
2. The entries are written on filing cards or uniform slips of paper, one card or slip per entry, noting the typescript page number on each entry in pencil.
3. The cards or slips are kept in the order in which the entries appear in the typescript (and number them consecutively, in case they are accidentally disordered) until the final version of the thesis is ready.
4. The cards or slips are processed with the final version of the thesis, and the final page references are inserted in pen on the cards or slips in place of the pencilled ones.
5. Only after the page-numbers of the final typescript have been inserted are the slips put in alphabetical order, any duplicates are removed and entries are combined where necessary.
6. Finally, the index is formatted in double columns, with a suitable font and line-spacing.

4.6 Final stages

4.6.1 Handing in the finished product

The thesis should be handed in to the appropriate body in the university (often the Registry or Secretariat) within the deadline which is normally allowed. This deadline is usually designed to allow the examiners a good chance to read and evaluate the work before the defence.

Ensure that the thesis has the correct size and the correct binding required by the norms of the particular university. The binding must often be of a specific colour. The stipulated number of printed and bound copies must handed in, and, of course, the candidate should keep a copy. The personal copy will help in the formulation of the presentation for the defence.

4.6.2 The defence

Normally, a public defence of a thesis lasts just over one hour. The candidate should bear in mind that he or she has all but obtained the academic title by this stage, so that this session should be viewed more as an opportunity to present the results to the public, often including family and friends, rather than as a gruelling examination. In the first twenty minutes or so, the candidate usually offers a synthesis of his or her dissertation and briefly presents the reasons for the choice of the theme, the particular difficulties encountered, and the originality and importance of the work. Finally the conclusions are presented. In the remaining period, the examiners question the candidate in turn, in such a way as to highlight important aspects of the work, to shed light on obscure details or to seek clarification of certain aspects.

Try to attend one or more defences prior to yours. Find out which other students are defending their research and sit in on their defence. In many departments this is expected of all graduate students. If this is not the case for you, check with your supervisor to see that you can get an invitation to attend some defences. At the defence try and keep your focus on the interactions that occur. Does the student seem relaxed? Observe the strategies the candidate adopts to keep calm. How does the student interact with the faculty? Does the student seem to be able to answer questions well? What would make the situation appear better? What things should you avoid? You can learn a great deal from sitting in on a defence.

Find opportunities to discuss your research with your friends and colleagues. Listen carefully to their questions. See if you are able to present your research in a clear and coherent manner. Are there aspects of your research that are particularly confusing and need further explanation? Are there things that you forgot to say? Could you change the order of the information presented and render it more understandable?

It's important that you have the feeling when entering your defence that you aren't doing it alone. Your supervisor should be seen as your ally at the defence. Don't forget, if you embarrass yourself at the defence you will also be embarrassing your supervisor. So, give yourselves both a chance to guarantee there is no embarrassment. Meet together ahead of time and discuss the strategy you should adopt at the defence. Identify any possible problems that may occur and discuss ways that they should be dealt with. Try and make the defence more of a team effort.

Don't be overly defensive at your defence! This is easy to say but sometimes hard to fulfil, if you have just spent a considerable amount of time on your research and there is a strong tendency for you to want to defend everything you've written. However, the examination board members bring a new perspective and may have some very helpful thoughts to share. Probably the easiest way to deal with new input is to say something like 'Thank you so much for your idea. I will be giving it due consideration.' There, you've managed to diffuse a potentially explosive situation and not backed yourself or the board member into a corner. Don't forget that your ultimate goal is to complete your degree successfully.

4.6.3 *Publication*

Publication of the whole or a part of the thesis after the defence often constitutes the final exercise required for obtaining the title of Doctor in a particular discipline. After the defence, the examiners usually furnish a series of directives as to what further work (if any) needs to be done, or what corrections need to be made, before the whole thesis or a suitable extract can be published. Having followed their suggestions, the candidate then prepares the text for publication, which usually involves a private printing operation by digital printing, or publication of an excerpt in a learned journal.[6] If the candidate prints the thesis privately in whole or part, he or she should adhere carefully to the norms of the university regarding the format, the cover page and the number of copies which must be handed in to the relevant authorities. In an ecclesiastical faculty, the *Imprimatur* and *Nihil obstat*, as an expression that the work is free from doctrinal or moral error, usually need to be obtained from the relevant authority prior to publication. Furthermore, it is wise to publish the thesis as soon as possible after the defence, while it is still fresh in the mind. Also, some universities require that after a certain period of time has elapsed since its defence, a thesis be re-submitted to its board of censors for fresh approval before publication.

6. Digital printing is a method which uses digital techniques in which the data and images are printed directly from a computer file (generally pdf) onto paper. The process differs from lithography, flexography, gravure, and letterpress printing.

5 REFERENCES

An apt quotation is like a lamp which flings its light over the whole sentence.

Letitia Elizabeth Landon, *Romance and Reality*

Notes are often necessary, but they are necessary evils.

Samuel Johnson, *Shakespeare*

The present chapter deals with the mechanics of making notes for essays, seminar and scientific papers and for theses. This method can also be adopted when writing a book in some academic field.

5.1 Footnotes and End notes

The term 'notes' as used in this chapter applies equally to footnotes and to end notes (namely references printed at the end of an article, chapter, or book). Notes are intended primarily for documentation and for the citation of sources relevant to the text. They can also be used to supply additional bibliographical material on the general subject being treated, so long as it is directly needed. They can also include extra expository material. All notes, whether or not they form complete sentences, should end with full-stops.

Wherever possible, a note reference number in the text body should be placed at the end of a sentence. Notes should be marked in the text by superscript numbers, with no punctuation (full-stops, parentheses, or the like), in sequence throughout an article or chapter.

A note reference number should follow any punctuation except a dash, which it should precede. It should appear at the end of a quotation, not following the author's name if that precedes the quotation. A note reference number in the text should never be repeated to refer to the same note; instead a new note is required. Do not attach a note number to a heading or subheading; an asterisk may, however, be used to indicate a general note to an entire chapter. Nor should a note number (or, indeed, an asterisk) be attached to the title of an article; a note attached to the first or last sentence, or an unnumbered note preceding the numbered ones, is preferable. Within the note area, the note indicator can either be in superscript like in the text, or else it can be in numerals the size of the footnote or end note text. The footnote or end note text should be generally 1 or 2 points smaller than the body text font.

Within the body of the text, references are numbered in sequence. A sequential numbering distinguishes the present method from that used in the natural sciences, where the numbers in the text are not in numerical order as they refer variously to the bibliography which is in numerical order. At least from an aesthetic point of view the present author feels that a sequential numbering in the text is preferable. The reference is indicated by a printed number at the end of the passage to which it refers. For an article, essay or term paper, the numbering continues from beginning to end. In a thesis or a book, numbering of references should begin again with each chapter. References are then indicated either with footnotes or with end notes.

5.1.1 Footnotes

Footnotes should be at the bottom of the text and they should follow each other sequentially in numerical order on the page. Each footnote number always corresponds to a footnote with the same number at the bottom of the page. Care should be taken that the footnote appears on the same page as the reference to which it is attached. A fundamental principle of scholarly work is that each page should be complete in itself. Some word-processing programs may have difficulty in achieving this, but ensure that even a long footnote at least begins on the page to which it refers. The beginning of the footnotes should be separated from the text by typing an unbroken line about three centimetres long, and then after a suitable space, the footnotes begin. Almost all word-processing programs make footnotes automatically.

5.1.2 End notes

An end note is placed at the end of a document. In a paper, this means at the end of the paper. In a thesis or book, the end notes are located at the end of each chapter. With a thesis, many universities only allow end notes if these are bound in a separate volume. It is wise to check the particular regulations of the relevant university before embarking on a choice between footnotes and end notes.

The actual text of footnotes and end notes should be single-spaced, but there should be suitable spacing between notes. Where two or more quotations in succession are from the same source and the same page, it is advisable to cover them all under a single reference. It is also possible to do this if the quotations are taken from different pages, but, in this case it is not always clear to the reader exactly what comes from where. Thus, in this latter situation, the pages must be cited in order of appearance.

Example:

> 'The ultimate synthesis,' Jaki notes, 'the rock-bottom layer of the material world, is today as far away as it has ever been.' However he qualifies this, lest he appear to support a sort of agnostic scepticism, by adding that 'the kernel of scientific truth will become better defined as time goes on'.[5]
>
> 5. S. L. Jaki, *The Relevance of Physics* (Edinburgh: Scottish Academic Press, 1992[2]), pp. 187, 137.

Note that the superscript '2' after the date of publication indicates the second edition of the book.

5.2 Making quotations

5.2.1 Direct quotation

With a direct quotation it is necessary to copy what an author has said 'word for word'. A long direct quotation has to be placed on its own, otherwise it would be lost in the text. Thus, if the quotation is five lines or less in length, it is put in inverted commas in the text: if longer than five lines, it is put in an indented single-spaced section on its own, without quotation marks, in a style sometimes known as a block quote. With a direct quotation, it is necessary to copy exactly what the author has said, even if there is a mistake in spelling or syntax. Sometimes a quotation may include a word that is misspelled or inappropriate.

Example:

> The ship floundered [sic], then was gone.

The Latin *sic* (thus) can be inserted to indicate that you have exactly reproduced the original statement. This protects the writer of a thesis from critics who may otherwise think that the error was made in copying the passage. To 'flounder' is to 'thrash about awkwardly,' while to 'founder' is to fill with water and sink.

Examples of direct quotations:

(a) 5 lines or shorter:

> Particularly over the past thirty years, the mass media have been featuring almost daily the various warning signs in the current environmental crisis. Our Holy Father, Pope John Paul II in his message for peace of 1 January 1990 declared that 'we are not yet in a position to assess the biological disturbance that could result from the unscrupulous development of new forms of plant and animal life, to say nothing of unacceptable experimentation regarding the origins of human life itself.'[1]
>
> 1. Pope John Paul II, *Peace with God the Creator, Peace with All of Creation,* Message for World Day of Peace 1990, 7.3.

(b) longer than five lines:

> The healing-process of the entire cosmos is one which takes place slowly and silently. It finds its origin in Christ's redemptive act and began on the morning of Easter Sunday, as G. K. Chesterton powerfully illustrated:
>
> > On the third day the friends of Christ coming at daybreak to the place found the grave empty and the stone rolled away. In varying ways they realised the new wonder; but even they hardly realised that the world had died in the night. What they were looking at was the first day of a new creation, with a new heaven and a new earth; and in a semblance of the gardener God walked again in a garden, in the cool not of the evening but the dawn.[2]
>
> 2. G. K. Chesterton, *The Everlasting Man* (Garden City, New York: Image Books, 1955), pp. 216–217.

5.2.2 *Indirect quotation*

With an indirect quotation, the citation quoted in the main body of the text is not direct, and is therefore not put in quotation marks and thus, in the note, the indirectness of the quote is indicated by using Cf. (=confer). Cf. is used whenever it is desired to acknowledge a debt to someone else's thought, however remotely. Cf. is also employed when making a paraphrase of an author's thought or expressing a debt for a single idea or multiple ideas. Instead of Cf. it is also possible to use 'See'. Cf., 'See' or 'Further' may also be adopted to refer to points made earlier or later in the work. 'Cf.p.15 above' refers to an earlier point and 'Cf.p. 267 below' refers to a later point.

Example:

> Particularly over the past thirty years, the mass media have been featuring almost daily the various warning signs in the current environmental crisis. Our Holy Father, Pope John Paul II in his message for peace of 1 January 1990 pointed out the dangers involved in a manipulation of the origins of human life.[3]
>
> 3. See Pope John Paul II, *Peace with God the Creator, Peace with all of Creation,* Message for World Day of Peace 1990, 7.3.

5.2.3 *Further detailed information*

References are also used to give further, more detailed information illustrating points made in the text, or to offer definitions of specific terms. This information would interrupt the flow if you put it in the main body of the thesis, but in a note the reader can refer to it when he or she so desires.

5.2.4 *Translations*

If the translation of some author is quoted in the thesis, the text in its original language can be furnished in the note, if it sheds some particular light on the discussion. In this way, the thesis should be written exclusively in one language for tidiness, and any original foreign words are then referenced as necessary. It is necessary to state who is responsible for the translation. If the writer of the thesis is responsible, then in a note the expression [translation mine] within square brackets should be employed. If just a simple technical foreign phrase appears in the text, it is sufficient to put the English translation in the text, and the technical expression alongside it in italics and parentheses.

Example:

> Most likely in this case the life context (*Sitz im Leben*) of Psalm 23 was the coronation of a king in Jerusalem, or perhaps it was sung at covenant renewal ceremonies.

5.2.5 *Quotation within a quotation*

In the case of a quotation within a quotation, the 'inner' citation must be distinguished from the outer one by means of either (a) a different type of quotation marks, for example, " " as opposed to ' ' or else (b) by guillemets or angle quotes, like this « ».

Example:

> P. Haffner states that 'one such cosmologist is S. Weinberg who wrote: "I cannot deny a feeling of unreality in writing about the first three minutes as if we really know what we are talking about."'[4]

4. P. Haffner, *Creation and Scientific Creativity* (Front Royal: Christendom Press, 1991), p. 93. Cf. S. Weinberg, *The First Three Minutes: A Modern View of the Universe* (London: André Deutsch, 1970), p. 7

5.2.6 Author defined italics

If, within a quotation, a word or phrase is italicized which the author did not so emphasize, this fact should be indicated with the expression [italics mine] or [emphasis mine], within square brackets, in the note corresponding to the quotation.

5.3 References with examples

The principle in each case is to specify the document consulted in such a way that it cannot in any fashion be confused with any other similar document. The idea here is that the writer of a thesis is making his or her own life a little more difficult in order to make it easier for the reader! It is preferable to avoid the use of expressions involving f. and ff. like p.5f. (meaning page 5 and the page following) and p.5ff. (meaning page 5 and the pages following). The pages should be cited specifically.

5.3.1 Scripture references

Scripture references can generally be left in the text in parentheses, using standard abbreviations for the books of the Bible. The method recommended is to state the book of the Bible, followed by the chapter, then a colon and then the verse. Various quotations from the same book and chapter are separated by a comma and those from different chapters or books are separated by a semi-colon. Hence the reference (Rev 21:1, 5–6) signifies the book of Revelation, chapter 21, verses 1 and verses 5 to 6. The indication (Pr 9:1; Ws 7:27) invites the reader to consult the book of Proverbs chapter 9 verse 1 and the book of Wisdom chapter 7 verse 27. It should be ensured that in any one given piece of written work one consistent system of Scriptural abbreviations be followed. All other quotations should generally be referenced. In the case of a Scripture reference, a particular application is made of rule 2.2.14 in chapter two, and the full-stop is put beyond the bracketed reference.

Example:

> 'The spirit of the Lord, indeed fills the whole world, and that which holds all things together knows every word that is said' (Ws 1:7).

If there is a question mark or an exclamation mark at the end of the Scriptural passage, a full-stop can be added after the bracketed reference so as not to leave it 'hanging in the air' between two sentences.

Example:

> 'When I gave the earth shape, did anyone help me?' (Is 44:24).

5.3.2 Church documents

The name of the Pope, Vatican department, Council or bishop should be given and then the type and name of the document, the year in parentheses, followed by the paragraph number. Usually, paragraph numbers are given in Vatican documents. This is much more useful than citing page numbers as these latter differ according to the language edition and according to the translation.

Example:

> 1. Second Vatican Council, Dogmatic Constitution on the Church *Lumen Gentium* (1964), 10.

If this document were to being cited many times, it could be suitably abbreviation (and then it must appear in the table of abbreviations as in §3.2.2 above) so that the note would simply read:

1. *LG* 10.

Now consider this example:

2. Pope John Paul II, Apostolic Letter *Mulieris Dignitatem* (1988), 7.3.

The subdivision 7.3 is useful. It means the third paragraph in the section officially numbered 7.

Remember that, when making a citation from an ecclesiastical document, it is insufficient to put simply a reference to a collection thus, DS 1638. The source must be stated, as follows: Council of Trent, Session XIII, *Decree on the Most Holy Eucharist*, Chapter II as found in DS 1638.

Further examples:

A) Vatican document

1. Congregation for the Doctrine of the Faith, Letter *On certain questions concerning Eschatology* (1979), 5.

B) Document from Episcopal Conference

1. Bishops' Conferences of England & Wales, Scotland and Ireland, *One Bread One Body* (London: CTS, 1998).

C) Ecumenical documents

1. WCC Inter-Orthodox Consultation, Report *Orthodox Perspectives on Creation* (Bulgaria:1987).

5.3.3 Ancient Texts

A) Old Manuscript

1. MS Ashmole 1462, miscellaneous medical and herbal texts in Latin England (Oxford: Bodleian Library, late 12th century), ff. 9v–10r.

B) Classics

For well-known editions of classic texts, only the name of the edition and the date of the volume are necessary and so the translator, place, and publisher can be left out:

1. Horace, *Odes and Epodes* (Loeb Classical Library: 1978).

For less familiar editions, full bibliographic information is given:

1. Aristotle, *Politics*. Translated and edited by E. Barker. (Oxford: Oxford University Press, 1958).

C) Patristic series

2. Gerontius, *Vie de sainte Mélanie,* Sources Chrétiennes vol. 90 (Paris: Cerf, 1962).

D) Medieval author

3. St. Bonaventure, *Commentarius in II Librum Sententiarum Petri Lombardi,* distinction 1, article 1, question 2, in *S. Bonaventurae Opera Omnia* (Collegio San Bonaventura: Quaracchi, 1885), vol. II, pp. 20–22.

5.3.4 Books

The basic model format for citing books is the following, which we now apply to various cases:

1. A. B. Author, *Title of Published Book* (City of publisher: name of publisher, year), pp. xxx–yyy.

A) Book with one author

The initial(s) and surname of the author must be supplied. It is preferable just to cite the initials rather than the full Christian name as the latter may not always be easy to find. In any case, consistency would not allow the use sometimes of full Christian names and sometimes of initials. Then the title and sub-title of the book duly italicized, the place of publication (city and publishing house) and the date of publication should be furnished. The page number(s) are then listed.

Example:

1. P. Haffner, *Creation and Scientific Creativity: A Study in the Thought of S.L. Jaki* (Leominster: Gracewing, 2009), p. 70.

B) Single book, multiple publication

2. W. Farmwinkle, *Humor of the American Midwest*, vol.2 of *Survey of American Humor* (Boston: Interesting Press, 1983; London: General Press, 1988), p. 6.

C) Book with two authors

The initials and names of the authors must be given, the title of the book, the place of publication (city and publishing house) and the date of publication. The page number(s) are then listed. The order of authors' names must be given exactly as printed on the title page of the book.

Example:

1. J. D. Barrow and F. J. Tipler, *The Anthropic Cosmological Principle* (Oxford: Clarendon Press, 1986), pp. 79–80.

D) Book with many authors

When dealing with a book with more than three authors, instead of the names of the authors, AA.VV., which means various authors, can be adopted. If you actually know who the authors are, it is best to avoid AA.VV.. For several authors, the name of the principal author followed by et al. may also be adopted, et. al. being an abbreviation for *et alii* (masculine), *et aliae* (feminine) or *et alia* (neuter), in all cases meaning 'and others'. Then the title of the book, the place of publication (city and publishing house) and the date of publication are given. The page number(s) are then cited as usual. In the case where a particular editor is responsible for this kind of volume, his or her name should be cited. Remember that if a passage from an article by one author within a collection is cited, this author should be named first in the note. Thus, a clear distinction is made between a collection of essays in which each author is responsible for one part and a volume in which all the authors have written the whole.

Examples:

1. Pope John XXIII, *Discourse to the Pontifical Academy of Sciences* (30 October 1961) in AA.VV., *Discourses of the Popes from Pius XI to John Paul II to the Pontifical Academy of Sciences. 1936–1986* (Vatican City: Pontifical Academy of Sciences, 1986), p. 103.

2. P. Poupard (ed.), *Science et Foi* (Tournai: Desclée, 1982), p. 78.

3. O. Pedersen, 'Christian Belief and the Fascination of Science' in R. J. Russell, W. R. Stoeger, and G. V. Coyne (eds.) *Physics, Philosophy, and Theology: A Common Quest for Understanding* (Vatican City State: Vatican Observatory, 1988), p. 126.

4. R. Quirk et al., *A Comprehensive Grammar of the English Language* (London and New York: Longman, 1985), p. 217.

E) A work by a corporate author

Treat the organization as the author, and cite the name or a short version of it.

Example:

1. National Endowment for the Arts, *1997 Survey of Public Participation in the Arts: Summary Report*. Research Division Report, vol. 39 (Washington, DC: National Endowment for the Arts, 1998), pp. 38–41.

F) Book in a series

Example:

1. M. Schmaus, *God in Creation*, vol. 2 of *Dogma* (London: Sheed and Ward, 1995).

G) Work in a series, separately authored

Example:

1. J. Auer, Mystery of the Eucharist, vol. 6 of J. Ratzinger and J. Auer, *Dogmatic Theology* (Washington, D.C: Catholic University of America Press, 1995).

H) Multivolume work, single author

Example:

1. A. Noyes, *The Torch Bearers*, volume II *The Book of Earth* (Edinburgh & London: William Blackwood & Sons, 1925), pp. 374–375.

I) Multivolume work, separately authored

Example:

1. I. Gebara and M. C. Bingemer, *Mary, Mother of God, Mother of the Poor,* vol. 7 of *Liberation and Theology* (Tunbridge Wells: Burns and Oates, 1989), pp. 10–34.

J) Translated book

Example:

1. H. Rahner, *Our Lady and the Church,* translated by S. Bullough (London: Darton, Longman & Todd, 1961), p. 20.

K) Book with two different publishers

Example:

1. D. L. Sayers, *Gaudy Night* (London: Victor Gollancz Ltd., 1935; London: New English Library, 1975), p. 12.

L) Chapter in an anthology

Example:

1. P. Tillich, 'Being and Love,' in R. N. Anshen (ed.), *Moral Principles of Action* (New York: Harper & Bros., 1952), pp. 661–672.

M) Collected Works

Example:

1. R. Descartes, *The Seventh Set of Objections* in E. S. Haldane and G. R. T. Ross, *The Philosophical Works of Descartes* (Cambridge: University Press, 1972), vol. 2, pp. 325–344.

N) Dictionary

Example:

1. S. De Fiores and S. Meo, *Nuovo dizionario di Mariologia* (Rome: Paoline, 1985), p. 15

O) An introduction or preface of a book

Example:

1. P. Fussell, Preface to *The Great War and Modern Memory* (London: Oxford University Press, 1975), p. 35.

P) Book with missing bibliographic information

a) Book without given author

Here practice differs as to the procedure. I suggest that one should put Anon. (for Anonymous) as the author where none is available, also to show that one has not simply been careless in omitting the name.

Example:

1. Anon., *The World of Learning* (London: Europa, 1997), p. 46.

b) No given place of publication

Use the abbreviation n.p. if the place of publication is lacking.

Example:

1. F. Kiefer, *Fortune and Elizabethan Tragedy* (N.p.: Huntington Library, 1983), p. 16.

c) No given publisher

Use the abbreviation n.p. if the publisher is lacking. If both place and publisher information is lacking, use N.pl. and n.pub. as longer abbreviations.

Example:

1. J. Smith, *An author's tale* (N.pub.: n.pl., 1934), p. 35.

d) No given date

Use the abbreviation n.d. if the date of publication is lacking.

Example:

1. B. Bligh, *Cherish the Earth* (Sydney: Macmillan, n.d.), p. 10.

e) Known but not given

If the missing information is known but not given, it may be included in square brackets. If you're uncertain about the accuracy of the information, use a question mark. If a date is approximate, precede it with c. for *circa* ('around'). Especially for old works (pre-1900), missing publication information may simply be omitted.

Example:

1. T. Carter, *Shakespeare and Holy Scripture* (New York: AMS Press, [1970]).

2. [T. Norton, Thomas?]. *A Declaration of Favourable Dealing by Her Majesty's Commissioners for the Examination of Certain Traitors* (London: c. 1583).

5.3.5 Articles

The basic model format for citing articles is the following, which we now apply to various cases:

> A. B. Author, 'Title of article'in *Title of Periodical* vol. p/ issue q (Year), pp. xxx–yyy.

A) Article in a periodical

The initial(s) and name of the author must be given, the title of the article in inverted commas, the title of the periodical duly italicized, specifying also the volume number and year of the periodical. Sometimes, if the journal has pages which begin again for every month or every issue of a given year, it is also necessary to specify the number which indicates the particular issue within a given year: e.g. 17/1, where '17' is the volume number and '1' is the issue number. Also check carefully when the year begins for a given periodical; it is not always in January! If the periodical is published in more than one language edition or has a name that could be confused with another journal, the place of publication should be indicated in parentheses after the name of the periodical. The page number(s) are then listed.

Example:

> 1. J. Cardinal Ratzinger, 'Jesus Christ today' in *Communio* (Notre Dame) 17/1 (1990), pp. 68–69.

B) Article in a newspaper

The initial(s) and name of the author must be supplied, the title of the article in inverted commas, the title of the newspaper duly italicized, specifying also the precise date on which it appeared (day/month/year). The page number(s) are then specified.

Example:

1. P. E. Hodgson, 'A Duty to Share Knowledge' in *The Times* (27 April 1985), p. 10.

C) Article in an encyclopaedia or dictionary

The initial(s) and name of the author must be supplied, the title of the article in inverted commas, the title of the encyclopaedia duly italicized, specifying also the volume number and place and year of publication. The page(s) are then listed.

Example:

1. F. D. Wilhelmsen, 'Realism' in *New Catholic Encyclopaedia* (New York: McGraw Hill, 1967) Volume 12, pp. 110–111.

D) A book review

The writer of the book review must be specified, the title of the review (if applicable), and then the name of the author of the book reviewed, the title and details of the book and also where the review was published.

Examples:

1. P. M. Haffner, review of S. L. Jaki, *Chance or Reality and Other Essays* (Lanham: University Press of America, 1986) in *Gregorianum* 89(1988), p. 598.

2. C. B. Kaiser, Review of S. L. Jaki, *The Savior of Science* (Edinburgh: Scottish Academic Press, 1988), in *Theology Today* (1989), pp. 226–227.

3. Friar Scotus, 'The «Mediatrix» debate renewed.' Review of M. Miravalle, *Mary Co-Redemptrix: Doctrinal Issues Today* (Goleta, CA: Queenship Publishing Company, 2002), in *Inside the Vatican* (June–July 2002), pp. 62–63.

E) An anonymous magazine article

1. Anon., 'Preserving Life on Other Planets' in *The Economist* (29 July 2000), p. 79.

5.3.6 Poems

The initial(s) and name of the author must be supplied, the title of the poem in inverted commas, the title of the collection (duly italicized) in which it was found with the name of the editor, the publisher and the place and year of publication. The page number(s) are then listed. In addition, a line number (abbreviated by l.) can be given for a poem.

Examples:

1. G. M. Hopkins, 'The furl of fresh-leaved dogrose' l. 4, in *Poems by Gerard Manley Hopkins* (ed. N.H. Mackenzie) (London: The Folio Society, 1974), p.79.

2. J. Dryden, 'A Song for St. Cecilia's Day, 1687' in *The Oxford Book of English Verse* (Oxford: Oxford University Press, 1983), p. 216.

5.3.7 Drama

As with poetry, omit page numbers when citing classic drama. Instead, cite by textual division (act, scene, etc.) and line, with periods separating the numbers. However the numbers are formatted in the original, use Arabic numerals (1, 2, 3).

Example:

1. W. Shakespeare, *Julius Caesar*, 3.2.73–76.

You should only specify the edition if necessary.

Example:

1. W. Shakespeare, *Julius Caesar*. Edited by R. Ormsby (Naperville, IL: Source Media Fusion, 2006), 3.2.73–76.

5.3.8 Letter in a published collection

1. N. Machiavelli to F. Vettori (10 December 1513) in *Machiavelli: The Chief Works and Others*, translated and edited by A. Gilbert (Durham, NC: Duke University Press, 1965), vol. 2, pp. 927–931.

5.3.9 A Song

The initial (s) and name of the author must be supplied, the title of the song in inverted commas, the title of the collection or album in which it was found with the name of the publisher, and the place and year of publication. The songwriter is sometimes not the same person as the singer. It should be stated if the author is anonymous.

Example:

1. C. de Burgh, 'The Spirit of Man' in *Into the Light* (London: A & M Records, 1986).

5.3.10 A Film

If a film is mentioned in the notes, it should be specified by the title (italicized), the main country of production, the company which made it and the year.

Example:

1. *Angels* (USA: Walt Disney, 1994).

5.3.11 Archive Material

Here, you must indicate the nature of the document and the relevant date. The archives of the relevant institution should then be specified and finally the parameters which locate it in that particular archive as was seen in chapter one, §1.1.2. Enough information should be furnished for the reader to locate the document.

Examples:

1. Letter of Cardinal John Smith to Bishop Fred Jones, 28 September 1979. Archives of the Pontifical Council for General Welfare, Protocol N° 679/79; Position 401.

2. British Library, Additional MSS 410, ff. 7–9; 912, f. 10.

5.3.12 Theses and dissertations

The initial(s) and surname of the author must be supplied. Then the title and sub-title of the thesis duly italicized, the place of publication (city and university) and the date of publication should be given. The page number(s) are then listed.

A) Published thesis

1. P. Haffner, doctoral thesis *Christian faith in God the Creator in relation to Modern Science according to Stanley L. Jaki* (Rome: Pontifical Gregorian University, 1987), pp. 20–27.

B) Unpublished thesis

The author of the material should be mentioned, the place where and the date when it was written (so that it can be located, for example in a university library) as well as the fact that it is unpublished.

Example:

2. V. Hartley von Knieriem, unpublished thesis *Towards a Theology of Woman according to Paul Evdokimov* (Rome: Pontifical Institute Regina Mundi, 1995), p. 45.

5.3.13 A report

Example:

1. E. Mendelsohn, A report prepared for a conference on women: *A Human Reconstruction of Science* (Cambridge, MA: Radcliffe Institute, April 1972), p. 31.

5.3.14 Proceedings

Example:

1. AA.VV., *Proceedings of the 1985 State Fish and Wildlife Directors Conference*. 4–6 June 1985 (Washington, DC: U.S. Department of Commerce, National Marine Fisheries Service, 1986), p. 12.

5.3.15 A Map

Example:

1. E. Rühle, *Geological Map of Poland* (Warsaw: Geological Institute, 1986).

5.3.16 A Painting

Examples:

A) Paintings reproduced in book

1. C. Monet, painting *La Cathedrale de Rouen*, Washington, DC., National Gallery of Art, in R. Gordon and A. Forge, *Monet* (New York: Abrams, 1984), p.174.

B) Painting in museum

1. C. Monet, painting *Rouen Cathedral Façade* (Boston: Museum of Fine Arts).

5.3.17 An Interview

The name of the person interviewed should be mentioned, the date on which the interview took place, and also the medium on which it was recorded.

Example:

1. Interview with Rt. Rev. John Smith, Bishop of Appleford, 25th May 1989. Transcribed from MP3.[1]

5.3.18 Lectures

Example:

1. D. Perkins, Lecture 'Mrs. Gardner's Circle: T. S. Eliot' at Isabella Stewart Gardner Museum (Boston: 2 November 1989).

---

1. MP3 is short for *MPEG–1 Audio Layer 3*, a patented digital audio encoding format using a form of lossy data compression. It is a common audio format for consumer audio storage, as well as a standard for digital audio compression for the transfer and playback of sound on digital audio players.

5.3.19 Musical scores

Examples:

A) Published musical score

1. G. Verdi, *Rigoletto,* Melodrama in three acts by F. M. Piave, ed. M. Chusid, in *The Works of Giuseppe Verdi,* series 1, *Operas* (Chicago: University of Chicago Press, 1960).

B) Unpublished musical score

1. R. Shapey, Score 'Partita for violin and 13 players' *Special collections,* Joseph Regenstein Library, (Chicago: University of Chicago, 1966).

5.3.20 Videocassette

Example:

1. L. Olivier, videocassette *Hamlet* (New York: Two Cities Films Ltd, 1948), 155 min.

5.3.21 CD-Rom or DVD

Example:

1. J. Smith, 'Rabbit keeping' on CD-ROM *Wild Animals* (London: Hutch, 2001).

5.3.22 Electronic material

Recent years have seen a rapid growth in publishing on the Internet, and it has become more and more common to cite material published through this medium. Authors should exercise at least the same discretion in considering the accuracy, quality and value of material published on the Internet as they would for material published by more traditional means. Often material has been scanned onto a web site, and insufficiently checked. It is not uncommon for Internet resources to change location on the server to which they were originally published, and even for them to be moved to a different server, or to disappear completely. Internet publications will often prove harder to pin down than their print equivalents, but systems such as DOI (Digital Object Identifier) that provide persistent identifiers for information resources are now used widely.

As far as possible, one should follow the style used for printed publications, as detailed above. Clearly, classical pagination may not be specified for many online publications. Try to specify as far as possible what is available, like the number of the starting page and the number of pages in the document. The descriptive elements listed below may be a useful guide to what you need to record when citing an electronic document.

1. Name of author(s) if given.
2. Year or date or publication (or date site was created or updated).
3. Title of document.
4. Medium (if not online).
5. Title of web site or database.
6. Pages, sections or paragraphs (if given) .
7. Web address (if appropriate).
8. Date you accessed the site.

Information should be given in the following order: Author's name, Title of item, Title of complete work/ resource, Publication details (volume, issue, date), Full address (Universal Resource Locator (URL)) or DOI of the resource <in angle brackets>, Date at which the resource was consulted [in square brackets], Location of passage cited, if available. The basic model format for citing electronic material is the following, which we now apply to various cases:

A) E-Books

Use the descriptive elements listed in the example below to cite e-books. A URL is not required if an e-book is already downloaded.

1. A. Author and B. Author, *Title of e-book* (Place of Publication: Publisher, Date of original publication). Source <Web address> [accessed date if appropriate].

Examples:

1. L. Bass, P. Clements and R. Kazman, *Software Architecture in Practice.* (Reading, MA: Addison Wesley, ^{2}2003). Safari e-book.

2. T. Eckes, *The Developmental Social Psychology of Gender* (Mahwah NJ: Lawrence Erlbaum, 2000). netLibrary e-book.

3. J. L. Parpart, M. P. Connelly, and V. E. Barriteau (eds.), *Theoretical Perspectives on Gender and Development* (Ottawa: International Development Research Centre, 2000). <http://www.idrc.ca/en/ev–9419–201–1–DO_TOPIC.html> [accessed 21 May 2005].

4. J. N. Pretty, *Regenerating Agriculture: Policies and Practice for Sustainability and Self-Reliance* (Washington, DC: Joseph Henry Press, 1995). <http://www.nap.edu/books/0309052467/html/index.html> [accessed 12 June 2006].

5. S. O. Jewett, *The Country of the Pointed Firs* (1910; online edition, Bartleby.com, 1999), <http://www.bartleby.com/125/> [accessed 16 August 2008].

6. St. Augustine, *Confessions & Enchiridion*, translated and edited by A. C. Outler, 1955. (Dallas, TX: Southern Methodist Union), <http://www.ccel.org/a/augustine/confessions/confessions_enchiridion.txt> [accessed 10 October 2005].

B) E-Journals

B1) Article from full-text database

Full-text databases include ProQuest, EAI, and Wiley Interscience to name but a few. Remember that the journals in full text databases may be accessed using links from library web catalogues. Once linked to the journal, check the screen to see if it is from a database. Journals in full text databases are usually not free on the Internet but are purchased on subscription by the library. For this reason the Database name is cited as well as the URL. When including the Internet address, it is best to use the recommended URLs for full-text databases, which are the URLs for the main entrance to the service and are easier to reproduce.

Use the descriptive elements listed in the model formula below to cite journal articles retrieved from full text databases. Pages are not numbered online, so only the first page is given.

1. A. Author and B. Author, 'Title of article' in *Title of Journal* volume number/issue number (year), inclusive page or paragraph numbers. Database name. <Web address of main entrance of the service> [accessed date].

Examples:

1. P. Fannin, 'Mechanical heart tested' in *The Age* (29 April 2002). Factiva. <http://global.factiva.com> [accessed 10 July 2004].

2. Mayor, S. 'Cloned calves are grown from cultured cells' in *British Medical Journal* 320 (2000), p.136+. ProQuest. <http://il.proquest.com> [accessed 30 June 2001].

3. Stelljes, K. B. 'Diagnosing the tough ones' in *Agricultural Research* 42/8 (1994), p.4+. Academic OneFile. <http://find.galegroup.com> [accessed 12 November 1999].

B2) Journal article from the Internet

Unlike journal articles from full text databases, these items are often freely available on the web. Some publishers offer recent issues for free and earlier issues for a subscription fee. Use the descriptive elements listed in the model below to cite journal articles retrieved from the Internet. When pages are not numbered online, only the first page is given.

1. A. Author, and B. Author, 'Title of Article' in *Title of Journal* volume number/issue number (year), inclusive page or paragraph numbers. <Web address> [accessed date].

Examples:

1. M. Goodacre, 'Fatigue in the Synoptics' in *New Testament Studies* 44 (1998), pp.45–58. <http://www.bham.ac.uk/theology/fatigue.htm> [17 July 1998].

2. S. Sohmer, 'The Lunar Calendar of Shakespeare's King Lear' in *Early Modern Literary Studies* 5/2 (1999), para. 3 of 17. <http://purl.oclc.org/emls/05–2/sohmlear.htm> [accessed 28 January 2000].

B3) Article accessed through an online database

4. J. Berger, 'A Post-Katrina Charter School in New Orleans Gets a Second Chance' in *New York Times* (17 October 2007), sec. B, <http://www.lexisnexis.com> [accessed 20 May 2008].

C) Internet Documents

Cite documents published on the Internet according to the specific type of document. Books, plays, government reports and company annual reports are examples of documents that may be published on the Internet. If no author or editor is given, simply supply the title. Use the descriptive elements listed in the model below to cite pages retrieved from the Internet.

1. A. Author, *Title: Subtitle*. Edition. Source or supplier information. (Date). <Web address> [accessed date].

C1) Online government publication

Example:

1. Canada. Office of the Auditor General of Canada and the Treasury Board Secretariat. *Modernizing Accountability Practices in the Public Sector* (6 January 1998). <http://www.tbs-sct.gc.ca/rma/account/oagtbs_e.asp> [accessed 10 October 2005].

C2) Short work from a larger website

Example:

2. St. Romanus (attrib.). 'The Akathist Hymn to the Blessed Virgin Mary' on *Catholic Online* (4 August 2002). <http://www.catholic.org/clife/prayers/akathis.shtml> [accessed 15 August 2002].

C3) Entire website

Example:

3. *Catholic Culture* on <http://www.catholicculture.org> [accessed 15 June 2010].

Further applications to other cases can be made using a development of the methods employed in the above examples.

5.4 Repeating quotes

5.4.1 When to use ibid

a) *Ibid.* is an abbreviation for *ibidem* which means 'in the same place'. It is employed when single references to the same work follow one another without any intervening reference.
b) *Ibid.* is used without any page number when the reference is found on the same page as the page reference immediately previous. A simple use is made of *ibid.* plus the page number if the page number is different from the previous reference.

5.4.2 When not to use ibid

a) Never use *ibid* when are referring to another reference by the same author. In this case Idem (meaning 'the same') must be employed, followed by the name of the work. For more than one author Iidem is used and for an authoress Eadem. Although Idem is a Latin word, it is not italicized so as to distinguish it from *ibid.*, which refers to a work.

Example:

1. S. L. Jaki, *Cosmos and Creator* (Edinburgh: Scottish Academic Press, 1980), p. 65.

2. Idem, *Is There a Universe?* (Liverpool: University Press, 1993), p. 70.

b) Never use *ibid* when there is an intervening reference between notes even though the reference has already been cited in full previously. In this case, the surname of the author may be employed (omitting his or her initials, unless another author in the thesis has the same surname), along with a shortened form of the work (which should be a complete phrase), omitting the publication details, and the page number.

Example:

1. P. Haffner, *Creation and Scientific Creativity: A Study in the Thought of S. L. Jaki* (Front Royal: Christendom Press, 1991), p. 70.

2. S. L. Jaki, *Cosmos and Creator* (Edinburgh: Scottish Academic Press, 1980), p. 65.

3. Idem, *Is There a Universe?* (Liverpool: University Press, 1993), p. 70.

4. Haffner, *Creation and Scientific Creativity*, p. 70.

c) Never use *ibid* when there are two references in the preceding footnote, as it will not be clear which one is being referred to. In this case, the successive reference must be written in full or in abbreviated form.

Example:

1. S. L. Jaki, *The Savior of Science* (Washington, D.C.: Regnery Gateway, 1988), p. 199 and see Idem, *The Purpose of It All* (Edinburgh: Scottish Academic Press, 1990), p. 144.

2. Jaki, *The Purpose of It All*, pp. 141–144.

5.4.3 When to use op. cit.

The expression *op. cit.* stands for *opus citatum*, meaning 'in the work quoted'. This may be used in the case of an author of whom only one work is being considered in the entire thesis. Then the work may be quoted in full the first time it is mentioned and thereafter *op. cit.* may be used. Some scholars also use the expression to stand for a title of a book which has been mentioned in the immediately preceding reference. If an author with several works is mentioned in the thesis, the first time an author is mentioned, each work should be cited in full. On subsequent occasions, only the surname and an abbreviated version of his work is given as described in §5.4.2, thus avoiding the use of *op. cit.*.

5.4.4 When to use loc. cit.

The expression *loc. cit.* stands for *locus citatus*, meaning 'in the place quoted'. The expression should only be used to replace quoting in full or abbreviated form the place where a quotation has been found, if there is no danger of confusion. Some scholars use it to stand for a title of an encyclopaedia or large reference work, or a page number which has been mentioned in the immediately preceding reference. This may not always be completely clear. It is, of course, possible to make references without the use of *op. cit.* and *loc. cit.* and many scholars prefer to avoid these expressions. If the method of abbreviating works laid out in §5.4.2 is employed, that system should not be mixed with a use of *op. cit.* and *loc. cit.*, because this shows a lack of economy. It is better to avoid superfluous expressions as far as possible.

5.5 Frequent mistakes

5.5.1 Confusing primary and secondary sources

Example:

Quoting St Augustine, Pope John Paul II states that the Eucharist in the Church is 'the Sacrament of piety, the Sign of unity and the Bond of charity'.[2]

2. Pope John Paul II, *Dominicae Coenae*, 13.5

The mistake is that St. Augustine should also have been mentioned in the note. So the correct way to make the note would have been:

2. Pope John Paul II, *Dominicae Coenae*, 13.5. See St. Augustine, *In Evangelium Ioannis tractatus* 26, 13 in *PL* 35, 1613.

5.5.2 Failure to cite primary source

Example:

As Jaki states: 'Without Creation, and a Creation by God who is Father, there is no possibility of a discourse about Incarnation, Redemption, and final Consummation in a New Heaven and earth, the great prophecy of the Creed.'[2]

2. P. Haffner, *Creation and Scientific Creativity: A Study in the Thought of S.L. Jaki* (Front Royal, Va.: Christendom Press, 1991), p. 61.

The primary source should have been put in the note and not the secondary source.

The note should have read:

2. S. L. Jaki, *Cosmos and Creator* (Edinburgh: Scottish Academic Press, 1980), p. 56.

5.6 Other methods of making references

5.6.1 Parenthetical Author-Page references

This streamlined format, used in the humanities, gives author and page in parentheses within the text of the paper, then sets out full references in a Works Cited (or Works Consulted) list. Developed by the Modern Language Association, it is now widely accepted in the humanities. The *MLA Handbook for Writers of Research Papers* gives detailed advice and examples on such matters as spacing of notes and Works Cited entries. It contains very useful sections on citing non-print sources such as films, paintings, sound recordings, and Internet sources. See also the MLA website for recommendations on details of referring to non-print sources (www.mla.org). The seventh edition of the MLA Handbook, published in 2009, has made a number of changes to the system. It specifies that every Works Cited entry must name the medium of the item, for instance, 'print' or 'web,' 'film' or 'DVD'. It advises that URLs do not need to be included for every Internet source, saying that readers can do their own search to find the current address. However, we suggest that students continue to include URLs for every Internet source. It continues to specify that for Internet sources you must include the date you read the page. That information lets your reader judge whether he or she is seeing the same version of the Web page you looked at. It now also specifies that if you read a journal article online through a database service such as Project Muse, you must give the name of the service.

Example:

> When Hamlet protests to his mother, 'Leave wringing of your hands' (III.iv.35), he is naming a universally recognizable gesture. As Smith says, similar broad physical

movements are 'still the most direct way of indicating inner turmoil' (960). Zygmundi confirms their continuing usefulness in contemporary productions of other sixteenth-century plays. Renaissance audiences would have recognized hand-wringing as a signal for inner distress (Brown, *Renaissance Stage* 111), specifically for a condition that the Elizabethan author Reynolds named 'ague of the spirits' (quoted in Mahieu 69). Poor sight lines in Elizabethan theatres also required highly visible body movements (Smith 964). In her new book, Brown attempts to show that such gestures are related to stylized movements from religious ceremonies, among other influences (Brown, *Ritual* 90). She argues that acting methods responded to both the physical conditions of the theatres and the audience's cultural expectations (Brown, *Ritual* 14).

Works Cited

Brown, Joan. *The Renaissance Stage*. Toronto: U of Toronto P, 1996. Print.

_______. *Ritual and Drama in the Elizabethan Age*. Toronto: Oxford UP, 2008. Print.

Mahieu, Aline. *Acting Shakespeare*. Toronto: Gibson, 2004. Print.

Shakespeare, William. *Hamlet, The Norton Introduction to Literature*. Ed. Alison Booth, J. Paul Hunter, Kelly J. Mays, and Jerome Beaty. 8th ed. New York: Norton, 2001. 941–1033. Print.

Smith, Jasmine. 'Renovating Hamlet for Contemporary Audiences.' *UTQ* 76 (2007): 960–69. Project Muse. Web. 21 Sept. 2009.

Zygmundi, David. 'Acting Out the Moralities for Today's Audiences.' Termagant Society Online. 31 Nov. 2002. Web. 22 Aug. 2009.

5.6.2 Parenthetical Author-Date references

The social sciences, management studies, and many sciences emphasize the author and date as the most important information about a source. The American Psychological Association (APA) has developed the most commonly used system. See the latest edition of the Publication Manual of the APA for very detailed advice on formatting a manuscript for publication. The APA website includes rules on reference formats for Internet sources (see www.apa.org).

This system uses only initials for authors' given names, does not use quotation marks or angle brackets, uses minimal capitalization for titles of books and articles, and italicizes volume numbers as well as journal titles. Strict APA format gives page numbers only for actual quotations (not for paraphrases or summaries), though some modified formats give them for all references. Ask your instructor when to provide page numbers.

Students using the APA system are usually asked to format their papers as if they were manuscripts being prepared for publication; that's why the examples here and in the APA Publication Manual don't look exactly like what you see in journals or books. The example below follows APA manuscript format.

Example:

> A group of statisticians, for instance, has re-analysed published data and argued that the compound words claimed as inventions of one chimpanzee are only the results of repeated random juxtapositions (Tannenbaum, Leung, Sudha, & White, 1996). Even more damagingly, Pinker (1994) summarizes the skepticism of various original researchers and observers about whether the signs produced in the Washoe project were really American Sign Language. His conclusion is that chimpanzees' abilities at 'anything one would want to call language' (p. 339) are almost nil. Experiments being conducted by Zelasko (2006) have so far failed to confirm the results originally claimed for chimpanzee learning of compound words.

References

Pinker, S. (1994). *The language instinct: How the mind creates language.* New York: Morrow.

Tannenbaum, R. V., Leung, K., Sudha, J. R., & White, M. A. (1996). *A re-examination of the record: Pitty Sing's creation of compound words. Journal of Biostatistics, 9,* 368–396.

Zelasko, J. (2006). *Learning and teaching words: Guided language acquisition among chimpanzees. American Psychologist, 57,* 750–765. Retrieved 20 September 2009, from http://www.apa.org/journals/ap57/zelasko.html.

5.6.3 Numbered note systems

Many theoretical and applied sciences use a citation-sequence system. They give numbered notes in the text of the paper that match a numbered list of sources at the end—given in the sequence the sources were mentioned, not in alphabetical order as in most other systems. Look at copies of journals in your discipline to see formatting details, including distinctive punctuation, compressed spacing, and lack of underlining or italics. Your professor may ask you to adopt the format used in a specific journal.

The system worked out by the Institute of Electrical and Electronics Engineers (IEEE) is often used in Computer Science and Engineering. Another very compressed system was created at a 1978 meeting of international medical-journal editors (ICMJE) in Vancouver. These Uniform Requirements for Manuscripts Submitted to Biomedical Journals are widely used (with variations) in the life sciences and medical sciences. Model your entries on what you see in journal articles in those fields, or consult the detailed guide prepared by the National Institutes of Health. The Council of Science Editors includes this system among others in its manual, *Scientific Style and Format.* The first example below adopts the system developed by the ICMJE.

Example 1:

Gastrointestinal symptoms in some patients have been found to be related to specific life crises (1, 2) such as marriage, retirement, or bereavement. Nausea in particular often lacks an organic cause (1, 3), but can be correlated with stressful events. A recent large-scale study of Danish medical records (4) found that 84% of cases of reported nausea were not resolved by medical treatment.

References

(1) You CH, Lee KY, Chey RY, Menguy R. *Electrogastrographic study of patients with unexplained nausea, bloating and vomiting. Gastroenterology* 2006;79:311–4.

(2) Dauphin J, Colomba J. *Nausea as symptom in school-entering children*. Sodeman WA, editor. *Stress-related illness*. Copenhagen: Munksgaard; 2009.

(3) Seaman WB. *The case of the pancreatic pseudocyst. Hospital Practice* 2008 Sept;16(9):24–5.

(4) Sodeman WA. *Most reported nausea not medically resolved. Family practice research updates* [serial online] 2008 Aug (cited 2008 Sep 16];7(8):[6 screens]. Available from: http://www.hosp.da/res/vol4/aug.html

Example 2:

'Iceland Moss: *Cetraria islandica*'

Edible Uses

A jelly is made by boiling the whole plant. It is nutritious and medicinal [4, 9, 10]. Rather bitter, it requires leaching, which can be done by changing the cooking water once or twice during the cooking process [12]. The dried and powdered plant can be mixed with wheat and used in making bread [2, 8, 10]. It is very bitter and the process required to leach it is far too time-consuming and tedious to be countenanced [6].

Medicinal Uses

Iceland moss has been used since ancient times as a cough remedy and has also been used in European folk medicine as a cancer treatment [14]. In present day herbalism it is highly prized for its strongly antibiotic and demulcent actions, being used especially to soothe the mucous membranes of the chest, to counter catarrh and calm dry and paroxysmal coughs—it is particularly helpful as a treatment for elderly people [14]. Iceland moss has both a demulcent and a bitter tonic effect within the gut—a combination almost unique amongst medicinal herbs [14]. The whole plant is strongly antibiotic, anti emetic, strongly demulcent, galactogogue, nutritive and tonic [3, 5, 6, 7, 8, 10, 11, 13, 14]. It is excellent when used internally in the treatment of chronic pulmonary problems, catarrh, dysentery, chronic digestive disturbances (including irritable bowel syndrome and food poisoning) and advanced tuberculosis [3, 14]. Externally, it is used in the treatment of boils, vaginal discharges and impetigo [13]. The plant can be harvested as required throughout the year [5], preferably during dry weather, and can also be dried for later use[6]. Use with caution [7].

Other Uses

A powerful antibiotic can be obtained from the plant and this has become a fundamental ingredient in a wide range of commercially produced disinfectants [5]. A brown dye is obtained from the plant [8, 10].

Cultivation details

There is no known information on the cultivation of this plant [13]. It requires clean air and is very intolerant of atmospheric pollution so cannot be grown in towns [13]. See the plants native habitat above for ideas on how it can be encouraged to grow [1]. This species is a lichen, which is actually a symbiotic association of two different species, one an algae and the other a fungus. It is very slow-growing [6]. This plant is often used in commercially produced disinfectants [5].

Propagation

The only way of reproducing this plant is vegetatively. Almost any part of the plant can be used to produce a new plant, simply separate a portion and place it in its new home.

References

[1] Fern, K. Notes from observations, and on field trips.

[2] Hedrick, U. P. *Sturtevant's Edible Plants of the World.* Dover Publications, New York 1972.

[3] Grieve, M. *A Modern Herbal.* Penguin, London 1984.

[4] Mabey, R. *Food for Free.* Collins, London 1974.

[5] Chiej, R. *Encyclopaedia of Medicinal Plants.* MacDonald, Edinburgh 1984.

[6] Launert, E. *Edible and Medicinal Plants.* Hamlyn, London 1981.

[7] Lust, J. *The Herb Book.* Bantam Books, New York 1983.

[8] Uphof, J. C. Th. *Dictionary of Economic Plants.* Engelmann, Weinheim 1959.

[9] Harris, B. C. *Eat the Weeds.* Pivot Health, Brentwood, TN 1973.

[10] Usher, G. *A Dictionary of Plants Used by Man.* Constable, London 1974.

[11] Mills, S. Y. *The Dictionary of Modern Herbalism.* Healing Arts Press, Rochester, VT 1988.

[12] Schofield, J. J. *Discovering Wild Plants: Alaska, Western Canada and the Northwest.* Alaska Northwest Books, Anchorage 2000.

[13] Bown, D. *Encyclopaedia of Herbs and their Uses.* Dorling Kindersley, London 1995.

[14] Chevallier, A. *The Encyclopedia of Medicinal Plants.* Dorling Kindersley, London 1996.

6 BIBLIOGRAPHY

Thousands kiss the book's outside who ne'er look within.

William Cowper, *Expostulation*

Books are the bees which carry the quickening pollen from one to another mind.

James Russell Lowell

6.1 General considerations

A bibliography is an alphabetical list of all materials consulted in the preparation of your work. Some principal reasons for supplying a bibliography would be, first, to acknowledge and give credit to sources of words, ideas, diagrams, illustrations, quotations borrowed, or any materials summarized or paraphrased. In this way, you indicate that you are respectfully borrowing other people's ideas. Second, a bibliography offers additional information to your readers who may wish to further pursue your topic. Third, you give readers an opportunity to check your sources for accuracy; an honest bibliography inspires reader confidence in your writing.

In general, the following elements must be included in a bibliography: the author of the work, its title, the place of publication, the publisher, the date of publication and solely for articles from magazines, journals, periodicals, newspapers, encyclopedias, or in anthologies, the page number(s). More detailed information is supplied with the examples later in the chapter.

Constructing a bibliography is based upon arranging names and titles in alphabetical or chronological order. Here are some fundamental rules about arranging names in alphabetical order.

6.1.1 Author

A) Two authors with the same surname

In the case of two authors having the same surname with the same initial, for example, John Smith and Jean Smith, the Christian names must be cited in full as these are used as a criterion to give precedence to Jean Smith.

Example:

Smith, Jean

Smith, John

If the initials are not the same, it should be clear that C. Smith has alphabetic precedence over C. A. Smith, and that C. A. Smith has alphabetic precedence over C. B. Smith.

B) Names with diacritical signs

It is important to know how to treat the case of letters which have signs connected with them such as:

é, è, ù, ç, ü, ö, ä, â, ê, ô, å, ñ, ø

These letters are considered for classification as if they did not have any sign. Thus Döllinger is placed after Dolcetto in a bibliographical list.

C) Names with a particle

In bibliographies, names with lower case particles are listed under the letter of the name proper, but those with upper case particles under the letter of the particle.

Examples:

da Silva under 'S' but Von Trapp under 'V'

In the case of names with a particle indicating the name of the father or the clan, apostrophes are disregarded in placing the allocation of alphabetical order.

Examples:

John McDermott goes under M, but is placed after Philip MacLean.

Daniel O'Grady goes under O.

Michael ap Owen goes under A.

Angela FitzHerbert goes under F.

D) Patristic and medieval names

During antiquity and into patristic and medieval times, family names were infrequent, and people were known by just one name. In this case, that one name will be the determinant for a bibliography. Sometimes, the person is known by their place of birth or origin, but in that case the name, rather than the place, is the important factor.

Examples:

The following authors all go under 'A':

Adam of Bremen

Adam of Cobsam

Adam of Eynsham

Adam of Perseigne

If there is a family name, on the other hand, that determines alphabetical order.

Examples:

St Thomas Aquinas goes under 'A'

Jean Buridan goes under 'B'

Thomas à Kempis goes under 'T'

Blessed John Duns Scotus goes under 'S'

With Hebrew names, which begin with an expression 'Ben' meaning son of, the alphabetical order is determined by the second part of the family name. Thus.

Ben Aron

Ben Moshe

A particular difficulty arises with Arab names, which are transliterated in any case. A consistent rule to follow would be that family names keep the al-/el-/ibn- attached to the rest of the family name at all times (whether there is a hyphen or not) and when alphabetizing is called for, whether in an index or bibliography, the al-/el-/ibn are an integral part of the list.

E) Titles

Titles of sanctity or of ecclesiastical or civil rank do not affect alphabetical order.

Examples:

Pope Saint Gregory the Great goes under G

Blessed Bishop Niels Stensen goes under S.

Sir Isaac Newton goes under N.

Titles of religious life are usually omitted from bibliographies. Thus for Fr Réginald Garrigou-Lagrange, OP, the entry should go under 'G' and would read:

Example:

Garrigou-Lagrange, R.

A difficulty arises, when you have several saints with the same baptismal or religious name, and here the principles from the previous section must be employed.

Examples:

St John Chrysostom

St John of the Cross

St John of God

St John Damascene

Here St John of God and St John of the Cross are listed under 'J' and the first significant word after 'John' determines their order. St John Chrysostom goes under 'C' because he is so often identified by the epithet 'Chrysostom'. While with St John Damascene the name really means St John of Damascus, and he is so often identified by the place, that he is put under 'D'. Thus the list would become:

Chrysostom, St John

Damascene, St John

John of the Cross, St

John of God, St

F) Noble names

Noble names and others formed by articles and prepositions follow specific rules. The main rule is that such articles and prepositions do not determine alphabetical order.

Examples:

Hans Urs von Balthasar goes under B.

Ignace de la Potterie goes under P.

However, Richard Van Dyck goes under V because the word 'Van' begins with a capital letter, is not a preposition, and is thus considered part of the surname. A further exception is that in Italy, articles and prepositions do determine alphabetical order. Hence F. de Santis precedes G. de Santo, but both are listed under the letter D. In French names of noble origin, care must be taken to see whether particles are attached to the name as this determines where a name may be placed in a bibliography.

Example:

La Bruvière
La Coste
La Montagne
La Monte
La Roche
La Vine
LaBach
LaBoon
LaBrecque
LaCharité
LaFabre
LaFontaine
LaPage

G) Double-barrelled names

There is an international rule which stipulates that generally the first significant surname governs alphabetical order, whether there is hyphenation or not. Care should be taken however, since while in Spain the first surname is important for alphabetical order, in Portugal the last surname gives the order.

Examples:

H. Hamilton-Dalrymple goes under H.

C. Maxwell Stewart goes under M.

It should be clear that J. Maxwell has alphabetic precedence over C. Maxwell Stewart.

Example:

M. Schmidt von Braun goes under S.

Some Japanese and Chinese names are presented with the surname first, so be careful when arranging these in a bibliography list. Spanish and Portuguese names are composed of two family names (mother's and father's) but are set up differently. In Spanish you have:
John <father's surname> <mother's surname>

Example:

Juan López Rodríguez is put under 'L' for López for the bibliography.

In Portuguese you have:
John <mother's surname> <father's surname>

Examples:

João Rodrigues Lopes goes under 'L' as Lopes is the last surname which is used for the bibliography.

Duarte Nuno Queiroz de Barros da Cunha goes under 'C' for Cunha.

H) Citing the author

When citing the author, use the surname and then the initials. This is the inverse of the citation method in the references, as seen in the last chapter. Unlike reference citations, after the author name, there is no comma in the bibliography. If the author is known only an author name without initials, there is a full-stop before the title of the work, otherwise with initials, there is just a single space.

Examples:

Aristotle. *Politics*.

Haffner, P. *Creation and Scientific Creativity: A Study in the Thought of S. L. Jaki*.

What is happening here is that to be totally consistent, one should put two full-stops after 'Haffner, P' in the second example, but that would look clumsy and unaesthetic, so the two full-stops are reduced by convention to only one.

With more than one author, it is important to use the authors' names exactly as they are found in on the cover page of the work. Within the list of author's names, it should be seen that the order is often not alphabetical, but is in order of importance. Hence, it is the first name of a list of common authors of a work which determines alphabetical order in a bibliographical list of works.

Example:

Roman, E., Beral, V., Carpenter L., Watson A., Barton C., Ryder H., et al. 'Childhood leukaemia in the West Berkshire and Basingstoke and North Hampshire District Health Authorities in relation to nuclear establishments in the vicinity'.

In this case, the article is placed under 'R'.

6.1.2 Title and subtitle

If the title on the front cover or spine of the book differs from the title on the title page, transcribe the title on the title page for the bibliography. Underline the title and subtitle of a book, magazine, journal, periodical, newspaper, or encyclopedia. Do not underline the title and subtitle of an article in a magazine, journal, periodical, newspaper, or encyclopedia; put the title and subtitle between quotation marks: Capitalize the first word of the title, the first word of the subtitle, as well as all important words except for articles, prepositions, and conjunctions. Use lower case letters for conjunctions such as and, because, but, and however; for prepositions such as in, on, of, for, and to; as well as for articles: a, an, and the, unless they occur at the beginning of a title or subtitle, or are being used emphatically. Separate the title from its subtitle with a colon (:).

Example:

Creation and Scientific Creativity: A Study in the Thought of S. L. Jaki.

6.1.3 Place of publication

Generally the place of publication is only required for larger works and books. It is not generally necessary to indicate the place of publication when citing articles from major encyclopedias, magazines, journals, or newspapers. Sometimes it will also be needed for magazines or journals to specify the particular case more clearly where it may be confused with another publication.

Do not use the name of a country, state, province, or county as a place of publication; use only the name of a city or of a town. Choose the first or principal city or town listed if more than one place of publication are indicated in the book. If the city is well known, it is not necessary to add the State or Province after it. Where the city or town is not well known, or if there is a chance that the name of the city or town may create confusion, add the abbreviated letters for State, Province, or Territory after it for clarification.

Examples:

Austin, TX: Englewood Cliffs, NJ: London, ON: Medicine Hat, AB:

6.1.4 Publisher

The publisher is generally only required for larger works and not for articles. Ensure that you supply the publisher, not the printer. If a book has more than one publisher, not one publisher with multiple places of publication, list the publishers in the order given each with the corresponding years of publication.

Example:

Conrad, J. *Lord Jim*. New York: Doubleday, 1920; New York: Signet, 1981.

If possible, shorten the Publisher's name. Omit articles A, An, and The, and skip descriptions such as Press, Publishers, and the like.

Example:

Use Macmillan, not Macmillan Publishing Co., Inc.

6.1.5 Date of publication

For a book, furnish the copyright year as the date of publication. However, do not draw the symbol © for copyright, or add the word Copyright in front of the year.

Example:

2005, not ©2005 or Copyright 2005

Use the most recent Copyright year if two or more years are listed.

Example:

In the book you see ©1988, 1990, 2005. Use 2005.

Do not confuse date of Publication with date of Printing, like 7th Printing 2005, or Reprinted in 2005. These are not publication dates.
For a monthly or quarterly publication use the month and year, or the season and year. If no months are stated, use Spring, Summer, Fall, Winter, as given.

Examples:

Alternatives Journal Spring 2005; *Classroom Connect* December 2004/January 2005; *Discover* July 2004; *Scientific American* May 2004.

For a weekly or daily publication use the date, month, and year.

Example:

Newsweek 29 September 2004.

6.2 Examples

Begin typing your bibliography flush to the left margin. Indent one centimetre for the second and subsequent lines of citation. Ensure the second and subsequent lines are indented automatically, and continue with the citation. Some citations are short and may fit all on one line. The bibliography text should be generally about one point smaller than the body text font.

A distinction should be made between primary sources, which constitute the work of a particular author, and secondary sources which consist of what other commentators have written about this author. Thus, within the following headings, the bibliography can be further divided according to the criteria of primary and secondary sources.

6.2.1 Sacred Scripture

It is neither necessary nor sufficient to simply write the Bible under this heading, because it is clear that in any theological work, the Bible will play some part! In fact, in a thesis which is not specifically specialized in Scripture, the particular version of the Bible which has been used should have already been mentioned in the table of abbreviations (see §3.2.2). This is important, because the particular edition of the Scriptures adopted will determine which abbreviations are used for biblical books. The Scriptural bibliography as such should be subdivided according to critical editions, synopses, dictionaries, concordances and translations of Scripture. The author(s), the titles (duly italicized) the place(s) and date of publication should be indicated. Next to the publication date, a superscript number indicates the edition. Under each sub-heading, the titles should be arranged alphabetically according to the surname of the principal author. For several works by the same author, the arrangement is chronological, with the oldest listed first. An often repeated source can simply be put in the table of abbreviations. For further ideas on how to organize a Scriptural bibliography in a thesis in a biblical specialization, the student should consult:

Elenchus Bibliographicus Biblicus of Biblica. Rome: Biblical Institute Press. 65 volumes up to 1984.

Elenchus of Biblica. Roma: Editrice Pontificio Istituto Biblico. 23 volumes up to 2007.

A) Critical Editions

Examples:

Aland, K., Black, M., Martini, C. M., Metzger, B. M., Wikgren, A. *The Greek New Testament*. New York/London/ Edinburgh/ Amsterdam/Stuttgart: 1975^{3}.

Nestle, E. and Aland, K. *Novum Testamentum graece et latine*. Stuttgart: 1963^{25}.

B) Biblical dictionaries

Examples:

Douglas, J. D., and Tanney Merrill, C. *The NIV compact dictionary of the Bible*. Grand Rapids: Zondervan, 1989.

Green, J. B., McKnight, S., Marshall, I. H. *Dictionary of Jesus and the Gospels*. Leicester: Intervarsity Press, 1992.

Hennig, K. *Jerusalemer Bibel-Lexikon*. Stu-Neuhausen: Hänssler, 1989.

6.2.2 Church documents

Documents of the Magisterium are arranged in the following order: First any collections of documents. Well-known and often-used collections of Papal documents like those arranged by Neuner and Dupuis or Denzinger and Schönmetzer should not be placed here, but rather should go in the table of abbreviations. Then, Papal documents are placed in chronological order, oldest first, so that the bibliography follows an historical order. For each Pope, the documents are arranged in chronological order, oldest first.

Examples:

AA.VV. *Discourses of the Popes from Pius XI to John Paul II to the Pontifical Academy of Sciences*. 1936–1986. English edition edited by Fr. Paul Haffner. *Pontificiae Academiae Scientiarum Scripta Varia* 66. Vatican City: Pontificia Academia Scientiarum, 1986.

Pope Pius XI. Motu Proprio *In multis solaciis*. *AAS* 28 (1936), pp. 421–424.

Pope Pius XII. *Allocutio—iis qui interfuerunt Conventui universali de Astronomia, Romae habito*. *AAS* 44 (1952), pp. 732–739.

Pope Paul VI. *Credo of the People of God*. 30 June 1968. Introduction, para 5. *AAS* 60 (1968), p. 435.

________. *Allocution on the Apollo 10 Mission*. 21 May 1969. *IP* 7 (1969), pp. 489–492.

________. *Allocution at General Audience*. 9 February 1977. *IP* 15 (1977), pp. 141–143.

Pope John Paul II. Encyclical Letter *Redemptor Hominis*. 4 March 1979. *IG* 2/1 (1979), pp. 550–609.

Further examples:

A) Vatican document

Congregation for the Doctrine of the Faith, Letter *On certain questions concerning Eschatology* (1979).

B) Document from Episcopal Conference

Bishops' Conferences of England & Wales, Scotland and Ireland, *One Bread One Body*. London: CTS, 1998.

C) Ecumenical documents

WCC Inter-Orthodox Consultation, report *Orthodox Perspectives on Creation*. Bulgaria:1987.

6.2.3 Encyclopaedias and Dictionaries

If the works are specifically Scriptural or relate to the Magisterium, they should be gathered, in alphabetical order, under the headings above respectively, under an appropriate sub-heading of encyclopaedias or dictionaries. If the encyclopaedic works are more general, they should be organized under a separate general heading in alphabetical order according to the titles of the works.

Examples:

Gran Enciclopedia Rialp. Madrid: Rialp, 1971–1977. 24 volumes.

New Catholic Encyclopaedia. New York: McGraw Hill, 1967. 12 volumes.

6.2.4 Ancient Texts

A) Old Manuscript

Here the parameters of the manuscript are supplied, followed by a brief description, and then location of the manuscript, including the approximate date.

Example:

MS Ashmole 1462, miscellaneous medical and herbal texts in Latin England. Oxford: Bodleian Library, late 12th century.

B) Classics

For well-known editions of classic texts, only the name of the edition and the date of the volume are necessary and so translator, place, and publisher can be left out:

Example:

Horace, *Odes and Epodes*. Loeb Classical Library: 1978.

For less familiar editions, full bibliographic information is given:

Example:

Aristotle. *Politics*. Translated and edited by E. Barker. Oxford: Oxford University Press, 1958.

C) Patristic series

Here it is necessary to specify the collection, or critical edition, in which the patristic author is to be found.

Example:

Gerontius. *Vie de sainte Mélanie, Sources Chrétiennes* vol. 90. Paris: Cerf, 1962.

D) Medieval author

Here it is helpful to specify the collection, or critical edition, in which the medieval author is to be found.

Example:

St. Bonaventure. *Commentarius in II Librum Sententiarum Petri Lombardi* in *S. Bonaventurae Opera Omnia*. Collegio San Bonaventura: Quaracchi, 1885.

6.2.5 Books

The standard formula for a book bibliography item is the following, which we now apply to various cases:

Author, A. *Title: Subtitle*. City or Town: Publisher, Year of Publication.

A) Book with one author

The initial(s) and surname of the author must be given. It is preferable just to cite the initials rather than the full Christian name as the latter may not always be easy to find. In any case, consistency would not allow the use sometimes of full Christian names and sometimes of initials. Then the title and sub-title of the book duly italicized, the place of publication (city and publishing house) and the date of publication should be supplied. If the title on the front cover or spine of the book differs from the title on the title page, use the title on the title page for the bibliography.

Example:

Haffner, P. *Creation and Scientific Creativity: A Study in the Thought of S. L. Jaki*. Leominster: Gracewing, 2009.

B) Single book, multiple publication

Example:

Farmwinkle, W. *Humor of the American Midwest*, vol. 2 of *Survey of American Humor*. Boston: Interesting Press, 1983; London: General Press, 1988.

C) Book with two authors

The names and initials of the authors must be supplied, the title of the book, the place of publication (city and publishing house) and the date of publication. The order of authors' names must be given exactly as printed in the title page of the book.

Example:

Barrow, J. D. and Tipler, F. J. *The Anthropic Cosmological Principle*. Oxford: Clarendon Press, 1986.

D) Book with many authors

When dealing with a book with more than three authors, instead of the names of the authors, AA.VV., which means various authors, can be adopted. For several authors, the principal author plus et. al. may also be used, et. al. being an abbreviation for *et alii* (masculine), *et aliae* (feminine) or *et alia* (neuter), in all cases meaning 'and others'. Then the title of the book, the place of publication (city and publishing house) and the date of publication are given. In the case where a particular editor is responsible for this kind of volume, his or her name should be cited. A clear distinction is maintained between a collection of essays in which each author is responsible for one part and a volume in which all the authors have written the whole.

Examples:

Pope John XXIII. *Discourse to the Pontifical Academy of Sciences* (30 October 1961). In: AA.VV., *Discourses of the Popes from Pius XI to John Paul II to the Pontifical Academy of Sciences. 1936–1986*. Vatican City: Pontifical Academy of Sciences, 1986.

Poupard, P. (ed.). *Science et Foi*. Tournai: Desclée, 1982.

Pedersen, O. 'Christian Belief and the Fascination of Science'. In: R. J. Russell, W. R. Stoeger, and G. V. Coyne (eds.) *Physics, Philosophy, and Theology: A Common Quest for Understanding*. Vatican City State: Vatican Observatory, 1988.

Quirk, R. et al. *A Comprehensive Grammar of the English Language*. London and New York: Longman, 1985.

E) A work by a corporate author

Treat the organization as the author, and cite the name or a short version of it:

Example:

National Endowment for the Arts, *1997 Survey of Public Participation in the Arts: Summary Report*. Research Division Report, vol. 39. Washington, DC: National Endowment for the Arts, 1998.

F) Book in a series

Example:

Schmaus, M. *God in Creation*, vol. 2 of *Dogma*. London: Sheed and Ward, 1995.

G) Work in a series, separately authored

Example:

Auer, J. *Mystery of the Eucharist*, vol. 6 of J. Ratzinger and J. Auer, *Dogmatic Theology*. Washington, D.C: Catholic University of America Press, 1995.

H) Multivolume work, separately authored

Example:

Gebara, I. and Bingemer, M. C. *Mary, Mother of God, Mother of the Poor*, vol. 7 of *Liberation and Theology*. Tunbridge Wells: Burns and Oates, 1989.

I) Translated book

Example:

Rahner, H. *Our Lady and the Church*, translated by S. Bullough. London: Darton, Longman & Todd, 1961.

J) Book with two different publishers

Example:

Sayers, D. L. *Gaudy Night*. London: Victor Gollancz Ltd., 1935; London: New English Library, 1975.

K) Chapter in an anthology

Example:

Tillich, P. 'Being and Love'. In: R. N. Anshen (ed.), *Moral Principles of Action*. New York: Harper & Bros., 1952.

L) Collected Works

Example:

Descartes, R. *The Seventh Set of Objections*. In E. S. Haldane and G. R. T. Ross, *The Philosophical Works of Descartes*. Cambridge: University Press, 1972.

M) Dictionary

Example:

De Fiores, S. and Meo, S. *Nuovo dizionario di Mariologia*. Rome: Paoline, 1985.

N) An introduction or preface of a book

Fussell, P. Preface to *The Great War and Modern Memory*. London: Oxford University Press, 1975.

O) Book with missing bibliographic information

a) Book without given author

Here practice differs as to the procedure. I suggest that one should put Anon. (for Anonymous) as the author where none is available, also to show that one has not simply been careless in omitting the name.

Example:

Anon. *The World of Learning*. London: Europa, 1997.

With several anonymous works, the first important word in the title determines alphabetical order. Should two anonymous works have the same first word, then they are classified according to the next important word in their title. Remember that A, An, and The are disregarded when alphabetizing the list of works cited.

Example:

Anon. *A Day in the Life of a Theology Student*. Rome: Newtext, 1993.

Anon. *A Day without Sunset*. London: Smallbooks, 1932.

b) No given place of publication

Use the abbreviation n.p. if the place of publication is lacking.

Example:

Kiefer, F. *Fortune and Elizabethan Tragedy*. N.p.: Huntington Library, 1983.

c) No given publisher

Use the abbreviation n.p. if the publisher is lacking. If both place and publisher information is lacking, use N.pl. and n.pub. as longer abbreviations.

Example:

Smith, J. *An author's tale*. N.pl.: n.pub., 1934.

d) No given date

Use the abbreviation n.d. if the date of publication is lacking.

Example:

Bligh, B. *Cherish the Earth*. Sydney: Macmillan, n.d..

e) Known but not given

If the missing information is known but not given, it may be included in square brackets. If you're uncertain about the accuracy of the information, use a question mark. If a date is approximate, precede it with c. for *circa* ('around'). Especially for old works (pre-1900), missing publication information may simply be omitted.

Examples:

Carter, T. *Shakespeare and Holy Scripture.* New York: AMS Press, [1970].

[Norton, T.?]. *A Declaration of Favourable Dealing by Her Majesty's Commissioners for the Examination of Certain Traitors.* London, c. 1583.

Note the use of the full-stop after the square brackets in the latter case

f) Two or more books by the same author published in the same year

The books are arranged in alphabetical order according to the first word(s) of the book title.

Example:

Gilbert, S. M. *Acts of Attention: The Poems of D. H. Lawrence.* Ithaca: Cornell University Press. 1972

Gilbert, S. M. *Emily's Bread: Poems.* New York: Norton, 1971.

Finally, the works should be organized in alphabetical order, according to author. Two books by the same author are put in chronological order starting with the oldest. If a work is a translation, the name of the translator should be indicated, but the book should be placed alphabetically under the name of the original author. Now we furnish an example of how to sort a list of books for a bibliography.

Example:

AA.VV. *Science and the Modern World* (Plenary Session held in March 1976) Part I. Pontificiae Academiae Scientiarum Scripta Varia 42. Vatican City: Pontificia Academia Scientiarum, 1976.

_______. *Scienza e non-credenza*. Vatican City: Segretariato per i non-credenti, 1980.

_______. *Science and the Modern World* (Plenary Session held in October 1978) Part II. Pontificiae Academiae Scientiarum Scripta Varia 49. Vatican City: Pontificia Academia Scientiarum, 1983.

_______. *Science and the Modern World* (Plenary Session held in November 1979) Part III. Pontificiae Academiae Scientiarum Scripta Varia 52. Vatican City: Pontificia Academia Scientiarum, 1984.

_______. *Scienza e Sapienza*. Atti della Solenne Commemorazione del primo centenario della morte di G. Gregor Mendel. Roma: I Rilievi, 1984.

_______. *Galileo Galilei: 350 anni di storia*. Studi e ricerche. Roma: Marietti, 1984.

Abrecht, P. (ed.). *Faith and Science in an Unjust World*. Vol. 2, *Reports and Recommendations*. Philadelphia, PA: Fortress Press, 1980.

Austin, W. H. *The Relevance of Natural Science to Theology*. London: Macmillan, 1976.

Balthasar, H. U. von. *Man in History: A Theological Study*. London: Sheed and Ward, 1968.

Barbour, I. G. *Issues in Science and Religion*. New York: Harper and Row, 1971.

Barrow, J. D., and Silk, J. *The Left Hand of Creation: the Origin and Evolution of the Expanding Universe*. New York: Basic Books, 1983.

Lambert, J. H. *Cosmological Letters on the Arrangement of the World-Edifice*. Translated from German, with an Introduction and notes by S. L. Jaki. New York: Science History Publications, 1976.

6.2.6 *Articles*

Articles should be organized in alphabetical order, according to author. Two articles by the same author are put in chronological order starting with the oldest. For an article from a newspaper, magazine, book or encyclopaedia, 'In' is used to denote the source. The standard formula for a book bibliography item is the following, which we now apply to various cases:

Author. 'Title: Subtitle of Article'. In: *Title of Magazine, Journal, or Newspaper* (Day, Month, Year of Publication), page number(s).

A) Article in a periodical

The initial(s) and name of the author must be specified, the title of the article in inverted commas, the title of the periodical duly italicized, specifying also the volume number and year of the periodical. Sometimes, if the journal has pages which begin again for every month or every issue of a given year, it is also necessary to give the number which specifies the particular issue within a given year: e.g. 17/1, where '17' is the volume number and '1' is the issue number. If the periodical is published in more than one language edition or has a name that could be confused with another journal, the place of publication should be indicated in brackets after the name of the periodical. The page number(s) of the whole article are then specified, not just the pages to which you refer in the endnotes or footnotes.

Example:

Ratzinger, J. Cardinal 'Jesus Christ today'. In: *Communio* (Notre Dame) 17/1 (1990), pp. 68–87.

B) Article in a newspaper

The initial(s) and name of the author must be given, the title of the article in inverted commas, the title of the newspaper duly italicized, specifying also the precise date on which it appeared (day/month/year). The page number(s) of the whole article are then specified, not just the pages to which you refer in the endnotes or footnotes.

Example:

Hodgson, P. E. 'A Duty to Share Knowledge'. In: *The Times* (27 April 1985), p. 10.

C) Article in an encyclopaedia or dictionary

The initial(s) and name of the author must be given, the title of the article in inverted commas, the title of the encyclopaedia duly italicized, specifying also the volume number and place and year of publication. The page number(s) of the whole article are then specified, not just the pages to which you refer in the endnotes or footnotes.

Example:

Wilhelmsen, F. D. 'Realism'. In: *New Catholic Encyclopaedia* (New York: McGraw Hill, 1967) Volume 12, pp. 110–111.

D) A book review

The writer of the book review must be specified, the title of the review (if applicable), and then the name of the author of the book reviewed, the title and details of the book and also where the review was published. The items are arranged in alphabetical order of the reviewer. If a reviewer is listed more than once their reviews are then placed in chronological order, oldest first.

Examples:

Haffner, P. M. Review of S. L. Jaki, *Chance or Reality and Other Essays* (Lanham: University Press of America, 1986). In *Gregorianum* 89 (1988), p. 598.

Kaiser, C. B. Review of S. L. Jaki, *The Savior of Science* (Edinburgh: Scottish Academic Press, 1988). In *Theology Today* (1989), pp. 226–227.

Friar Scotus. 'The «Mediatrix» debate renewed'. Review of M. Miravalle, *Mary Co-Redemptrix: Doctrinal Issues Today* (Goleta, CA: Queenship Publishing Company, 2002). In *Inside the Vatican* (June–July 2002), pp. 62–63.

E) An anonymous magazine article

Anon. 'Preserving Life on Other Planets'. In: *The Economist* (29 July 2000), p. 79.

Now we furnish an example of how to sort a list of articles for a bibliography.

Example:

Caldecott, S. 'Cosmology, eschatology, ecology: Some reflections on Sollicitudo Rei Socialis'. In: *Communio* 15/3 (Fall 1988) pp. 305–318.

Hodgson, P. E. 'A Duty to Share Knowledge'. In: *The Times* (27 April 1985), p. 10.

Jaki, S. L. Review of L. Bouyer, *Cosmos et la gloire de Dieu* (Paris: Cerf, 1982). In: *The Downside Review* 102 (1984), pp. 301–307.

Juric, S. Review of S. L. Jaki, *Genesis 1 through the Ages* (London: Thomas More Press, 1992). In: *Angelicum* 70/3 (1993), pp. 450–451.

Kasper, W. 'Hope in the final coming of Jesus Christ in Glory'. In: *Communio* 12/4 (Winter 1985), pp. 368–384.

McDermott, J. M. 'Catholic Doctrine on Death'. In: R. J. White, H. Angstwurm and I. Carrasco de Paula (eds.), *The Determination of Brain Death and its Relationship with Human Death* (Città del Vaticano: Pontificia Academia Scientiarum, 1992), pp. 153–176.

Ratzinger, J. 'Jesus Christ today'. In: *Communio* (Notre Dame) 17/1 (Spring 1990), pp. 68–87.

Wilhelmsen, F. D. 'Realism'. In: *New Catholic Encyclopaedia* (New York: McGraw Hill, 1967) Volume 12, pp. 110–111.

6.2.7 Poems

The name and initial(s) of the author must be supplied, the title of the poem in inverted commas, the title of the collection (duly italicized) in which it was found with the name of the editor, and the place and year of publication. The page number(s) are then listed. In addition, a line number (abbreviated by l.) can be given for a poem.

Example:

Dryden, J. 'A Song for St. Cecilia's Day, 1687'. In: *The Oxford Book of English Verse* (Oxford: Oxford University Press, 1983).

Hopkins, G. M. 'The furl of fresh-leaved dogrose' l. 4. In: *Poems by Gerard Manley Hopkins* (ed. N.H. Mackenzie) (London: The Folio Society, 1974), p. 79.

6.2.8 Drama

As with poetry, omit page numbers when citing classic drama. Instead, cite by textual division (act, scene, etc.) and line, with periods separating the numbers. However the numbers are formatted in the original, use Arabic numerals (1, 2, 3).

Example:

Shakespeare, W. *Julius Caesar*, 3.2.73–76.

You should only specify the edition if necessary.

Example:

Shakespeare, W. *Julius Caesar*. Edited by R. Ormsby (Naperville, IL: Source Media Fusion, 2006), 3.2.73–76.

6.2.9 Letter in a published collection

Machiavelli, N. to F. Vettori (10 December 1513). In: *Machiavelli: The Chief Works and Others*, translated and edited by A. Gilbert (Durham, NC: Duke University Press, 1965), vol. 2, pp. 927–931.

6.2.10 A Song

The name and initial (s) of the author must be given, the title of the song in inverted commas, the title of the collection or album in which it was found with the name of the publisher, and the place and year of publication. The songwriter is sometimes not the same person as the singer. It should be stated if the author is anonymous.

Example:

Burgh, C. de. 'The Spirit of Man'. In *Into the Light* (London: A & M Records, 1986).

6.2.11 A Film

If a film is mentioned in the bibliography, it should be specified by the title (italicized), the main country of production, the company which made it and the year.

Example:

Angels. USA: Walt Disney, 1994.

6.2.12 Archive Material

The material is arranged in chronological order, starting with the oldest.

Example:

Letter of Cardinal John Smith to Bishop Fred Jones, 28 September 1979. Archives of the Pontifical Council for General Welfare, Protocol N° 679/79; Position 401.

Letter of Sir John Jones to Mr. Alfred Johnstone, Chairman of the Department of Transport, Archives of the Department of Transport, Document N° 51643 of 1986.

6.2.13 *Theses*

A) Published thesis

The author of the material should be mentioned, as well as the place where and the date when it was published.

Example:

Haffner, P. Doctoral thesis *Christian faith in God the Creator in relation to Modern Science according to Stanley L. Jaki*. Rome: Pontifical Gregorian University, 1987.

B) Unpublished thesis

The author of the material should be mentioned, the place where and the date when it was written (so that it can be located, for example in a university library) as well as the fact that it is unpublished.

Example:

Hartley von Knieriem, V. Unpublished thesis *Towards a Theology of Woman according to Paul Evdokimov*. Rome: Pontifical Institute Regina Mundi, 1995.

6.2.14 A report

Example:

Mendelsohn, E. A report prepared for a conference on women: *A Human Reconstruction of Science*. Cambridge, MA: Radcliffe Institute, April 1972.

6.2.15 Proceedings

Example:

AA.VV. *Proceedings of the 1985 State Fish and Wildlife Directors Conference.* (4–6 June 1985) Washington, DC: U.S. Department of Commerce, National Marine Fisheries Service, 1986.

6.2.16 A Map

Example:

Rühle, E. *Geological Map of Poland.* Warsaw: Geological Institute, 1986.

6.2.17 A Painting

Examples:

A) Paintings reproduced in a book

Monet, C. Painting *La Cathedrale de Rouen.* Washington, DC.: National Gallery of Art. In: R. Gordon and A. Forge, *Monet* (New York: Abrams, 1984), p.174.

B) Painting in a museum

Monet, C. Painting *Rouen Cathedral Façade.* Boston: Museum of Fine Arts.

6.2.18 An Interview

The material is arranged in *chronological* order, starting with the oldest

Example:

Interview with Rt. Rev. Adam Hayforth, Bishop of Appleford, (25 May 1989).

Interview with Mr. Jon Yu, (27 April 1994).

6.2.19 Lectures

Example:

Perkins, D. Lecture 'Mrs. Gardner's Circle: T. S. Eliot' at Isabella Stewart Gardner Museum. Boston: 2 November 1989.

6.2.20 Musical scores

Examples:

A) Published musical score

Verdi, G. *Rigoletto,* Melodrama in three acts by F. M. Piave, ed. M. Chusid. In: *The Works of Giuseppe Verdi,* series 1, *Operas* (Chicago: University of Chicago Press, 1960).

B) Unpublished musical score

Shapey, R. Score 'Partita for violin and 13 players' *Special collections,* Joseph Regenstein Library. Chicago: University of Chicago, 1966.

6.2.21 Videocassette

Example:

Olivier, L. Videocassette *Hamlet*. New York: Two Cities Films Ltd, 1948.

6.2.22 CD-Rom or DVD

Examples:

Smith, J. 'Rabbit keeping' on CD-ROM *Wild Animals*. London: Hutch, 2001.

Stevens, G. (director). *A Place in the Sun*. DVD. Paramount: 2001.

6.2.23 Electronic documents

References to electronic publications begin with the same information that would normally be provided for a printed source. Additional information must be provided (depending on the type of electronic publication) to identify correctly the document that you accessed in an electronic format. An electronic publication could be an Internet site, a journal article published on the Internet, or a journal article retrieved from one of the full text databases available from a library. Some documents are published in both paper and electronic formats. It is important to cite according to the format you accessed.

Clearly, classical pagination may not be specified for many online publications. Try to specify as far as possible what is available, like the number of the starting page and the number of pages in the document. The descriptive elements listed below may be a useful guide to what you need to record when citing an electronic document.

1. Name of author(s) if given.
2. Year or date or publication (or date site was created or updated).
3. Title of document.
4. Medium (if not online).
5. Title of web site or database.
6. Pages, sections or paragraphs (if given) .
7. Web address (if appropriate).
8. Date you accessed the site.

A) E-Books

Use the descriptive elements listed in the example below to cite e-books. A URL is not required if an e-book is already downloaded.

Author, A. and Author, B. *Title of e-book*. Place of Publication: Publisher, Date of original publication. Source. <Web address> [accessed date if appropriate].

Examples:

Bass, L., Clements, P. and Kazman, R. *Software Architecture in Practice*. Reading, MA: Addison Wesley, ^{2}2003. Safari e-book.

Eckes, T. *The Developmental Social Psychology of Gender*. Mahwah NJ: Lawrence Erlbaum, 2000. netLibrary e-book.

Parpart, J. L., Connelly, M. P. and Barriteau, V. E. (eds.). *Theoretical Perspectives on Gender and Development*. Ottawa, Canada: International Development Research Centre, 2000. <http://www.idrc.ca/en/ev–9419–201–1–DO_TOPIC.html> [accessed 21 May 2005].

Pretty, J. N. *Regenerating Agriculture: Policies and Practice for Sustainability and Self-Reliance*. Washington DC: Joseph Henry Press, 1995. <http://www.nap.edu/books/0309052467/html/index.html> [accessed 12 June 2006].

B) E-Journals

B1) Article from full-text database

The Database name is cited as well as the URL. When including the Internet address, it is best to use the recommended URLs for full-text databases, which are the URLs for the main entrance to the service and are easier to reproduce.

Use the descriptive elements listed in the model below to cite journal articles retrieved from full text databases. Pages are not numbered online, so only the first page is given.

Author, A. and Author, B. 'Title of article'. In: *Title of Journal* volume number/issue number (year), inclusive page or paragraph numbers. Database name. <Web address of main entrance of the service> [accessed date].

Examples:

Fannin, P. 'Mechanical heart tested'. In:*The Age* (29 April 2002). Factiva. <http://global.factiva.com> [accessed 10 July 2004].

Mayor, S. 'Cloned calves are grown from cultured cells'. In: *British Medical Journal* 320 (2000), pp.136+. ProQuest. <http://il.proquest.com> [accessed 30 June 2001].

Stelljes, K. B. 'Diagnosing the tough ones'. In: *Agricultural Research* 42/8 (1994), pp.4+. *Academic OneFile*. <http://find.galegroup.com> [accessed 12 November 1999].

B2) Journal article from the Internet

Unlike journal articles from full text databases, these items are often freely available on the web. Some publishers offer recent issues for free and earlier issues for a subscription fee. Use the descriptive elements listed in the model below to cite journal articles retrieved from the Internet. When pages are not numbered online, only the first page is supplied.

Author, A., and Author, B. 'Title of Article'. In: *Title of Journal* volume number/issue number (year), inclusive page or paragraph numbers. <Web address> [accessed date].

Example:

Goodacre, M. 'Fatigue in the Synoptics'. In: *New Testament Studies* 44 (1998), pp.45–58. <http://www.bham.ac.uk/theology/fatigue.htm> [accessed 17 July 1998].

Sohmer, S. 'The Lunar Calendar of Shakespeare's King Lear'. In: *Early Modern Literary Studies* 5/2 (1999) <http://purl.oclc.org/emls/05–2/sohmlear.htm> [accessed 28 January 2000].

B3) Article accessed through an online database

Berger, J. 'A Post-Katrina Charter School in New Orleans Gets a Second Chance'. In: *New York Times* (17 October 2007), sec. B, <http://www.lexisnexis.com> [accessed 20 May 2008].

C) Internet Documents

Cite documents published on the Internet according to the specific type of document. Books, plays, government reports and company annual reports are examples of documents that may be published on the Internet. If no author or editor is given, simply supply the title which will determine its order in the list. Use the descriptive elements listed in the model below to cite pages retrieved from the Internet.

Author, A. *Title: Subtitle*. Edition. Source or supplier information. (Date). <Web address> [accessed date].

C1) Online government publication

Example:

Canada. Office of the Auditor General of Canada and the Treasury Board Secretariat. *Modernizing Accountability Practices in the Public Sector* (6 January 1998). <http://www.tbs-sct.gc.ca/rma/account/oagtbs_e.asp> [accessed 10 October 2005].

C2) Short work from a larger website

Example:

St. Romanus (attrib.). 'The Akathist Hymn to the Blessed Virgin Mary' on *Catholic Online* (4 August 2002). <http://www.catholic.org/clife/prayers/akathis.shtml> [accessed 15 August 2002].

C3) Entire website

Example:

Catholic Culture on <http://www.catholicculture.org> [accessed 15 June 2010].

www.ingramcontent.com/pod-product-compliance
Lightning Source LLC
Chambersburg PA
CBHW031246090426
42742CB00007B/331

* 9 7 8 0 8 5 2 4 4 7 4 3 7 *